BBC
goodfood
ONE-POT DISHES

D1390197

10 9 8 7 6 5 4 3

first published in 2006 by BBC Books, an imprint of Ebury Publishing
A Random House Group company. This revised edition published 2014.

Recipes © BBC Worldwide 2006
Photographs © BBC Worldwide 2006
Book design © Woodlands Books Ltd 2014
All the recipes contained in this book first appeared in BBC *Good Food* Magazine

The Random House Group Limited Reg. No. 954009

Addresses for companies within the Random House Group can be found at www.randomhouse.co.uk

A CIP catalogue record for this book is available from the British Library.

Penguin Random House is committed to a sustainable future for our business, our readers and our planet.
This book is made from Forest Stewardship Council® certified paper.

To buy books by your favourite authors and register for offers visit www.randomhouse.co.uk

Printed and bound by Firmengruppe APPL, aprinta druck, Wemding, Germany
Colour origination by Dot Gradations Ltd

MIX
Paper from
responsible sources
FSC® C018179
www.fsc.org

Edited by Barney Desmazery
Commissioning Editor: Lizzy Gray
Project Editor: Lizzy Gaisford
Designers: Interstate Creative Partners Ltd
Design Manager: Kathryn Gammon
Production: Alex Goddard
Picture Researcher: Gabby Harrington

ISBN: 9781849908658

PICTURE CREDITS AND RECIPE CREDITS

BBC *Good Food* Magazine and BBC Books would like to thank the following for providing photos. While every effort has been made to trace and acknowledge all photographers, we would like to apologize should there be any errors or omissions.

Carolyn Barber p85; Marie-Louise Avery p21; Iain Bagwell p25, p97, p113; Steve Baxter p51, p125, p163; Peter Cassidy p169; Carl Clemens-Gros p115; Ken Field p11, p13, p37, p43, p53, p67, p97, p139, p143, p171; Will Heap p71, p153, p207; Jonathan Kennedy p99; Dave King p131; Adrian Lawrence p107, p165; Jason Lowe p197; David Munns p6, p23, p31, p39, p45, p59, p61, p83, p101, p159, p167, p179, p185, p209; Myles New p145; Myles New & Craig Robertson p17; Stuart Ovenden p35, p47, p95, p175, p183; Lis Parsons p141, p149; Craig Robertson p27, p199, p203; Howard Shooter p49, p89; Sharon Smith p137; Roger Stowell p19, p33, p65, p73, p81, p91, p109, p121, p127, p133, p157, p155, p181, p191, p205, p211; Sam Stowell p75, p123, p129, p187; Simon Walton p173; Cameron Watt p161; Philip Webb p15, p29, p55, p69, p77, p79, p87, p93, p105, p135, p147, p151, p177, p195; Simon Wheeler p63, p189, p193, p201; Isobel Wield p57.

All the recipes in this book were created by the editorial team at *Good Food* and by regular contributors to BBC magazines.

goodfood
ONE-POT DISHES

Editor **Jeni Wright**

Contents

INTRODUCTION   6

Soups   10
Meat & poultry   32
Fish & seafood   88
Veggie-friendly dishes   136
Suppers for a crowd   164
Puddings & desserts   192

INDEX   212

Introduction

Making food you want to share with friends doesn't have to involve juggling lots of pans, and this revised and updated edition is the perfect collection to prove that some of the most delicious recipes are made in just one pot. Not only does one-pot cooking save time and washing up, it locks in all flavour and brings all the ingredients together to combine into one harmonious dish that you can serve straight from stove to table for everyone to help themselves.

Most of the recipes in this book are complete meals in themselves, like the *Fragrant courgette & prawn curry* pictured opposite (see page 100 for the recipe), so all they need to go with them is a quick-fix salad or some bread. Next time you're in the supermarket, take a look at the wide range of ready-cooked rice and noodles on offer – heating through is all they need.

As always at BBC *Good Food* magazine we've done the hard work for you – we've triple-tested each recipe so they'll work every time, and we've included nutritional breakdowns so you know exactly what you're eating. Last but not least, we've included a special chapter of our favourite puddings and desserts that we know you will love – and they're all one-pot too. How clever is that?

Jeni Wright

Jeni Wright
BBC *Good Food* Magazine

Notes &
Conversion Tables
· · · · · · · · · · · · · · · · · · · ·

NOTES ON THE RECIPES
- Eggs are large in the UK and Australia and extra large in America unless stated.
- Wash fresh produce before preparation.
- Recipes contain nutritional analyses for 'sugar', which means the total sugar content including all natural sugars in the ingredients, unless otherwise stated.

OVEN TEMPERATURES

GAS	°C	°C FAN	°F	OVEN TEMP.
¼	110	90	225	Very cool
½	120	100	250	Very cool
1	140	120	275	Cool or slow
2	150	130	300	Cool or slow
3	160	140	325	Warm
4	180	160	350	Moderate
5	190	170	375	Moderately hot
6	200	180	400	Fairly hot
7	220	200	425	Hot
8	230	210	450	Very hot
9	240	220	475	Very hot

APPROXIMATE WEIGHT CONVERSIONS
- All the recipes in this book list both imperial and metric measurements. Conversions are approximate and have been rounded up or down. Follow one set of measurements only; do not mix the two.
- Cup measurements, which are used in Australia and America, have not been listed here as they vary from ingredient to ingredient. Kitchen scales should be used to measure dry/solid ingredients.

Good Food is concerned about sustainable sourcing and animal welfare. Where possible, humanely reared meats, sustainably caught fish (see fishonline.org for further information from the Marine Conservation Society) and free-range chickens and eggs are used when recipes are originally tested.

SPOON MEASURES

Spoon measurements are level unless otherwise specified.

- 1 teaspoon (tsp) = 5ml
- 1 tablespoon (tbsp) = 15ml
- 1 Australian tablespoon = 20ml (cooks in Australia should measure 3 teaspoons where 1 tablespoon is specified in a recipe)

APPROXIMATE LIQUID CONVERSIONS

METRIC	IMPERIAL	AUS	US
50ml	2fl oz	¼ cup	¼ cup
125ml	4fl oz	½ cup	½ cup
175ml	6fl oz	¾ cup	¾ cup
225ml	8fl oz	1 cup	1 cup
300ml	10fl oz/½ pint	½ pint	1¼ cups
450ml	16fl oz	2 cups	2 cups/1 pint
600ml	20fl oz/1 pint	1 pint	2½ cups
1 litre	35fl oz/1¾ pints	1¾ pints	1 quart

Chunky winter broth

This hearty winter supper is a great way of getting your daily vitamins.

 20 minutes 4

- 2 x 400g cans chopped tomatoes
- 2 litres/3½ pints vegetable stock
- 4 carrots, sliced
- 2 x 400g cans mixed pulses, drained and rinsed
- 175g/6oz spinach leaves
- 1 tbsp roasted red pepper pesto
- crusty bread, to serve

1 Tip the tomatoes into a large pan along with the stock. Bring to the boil, turn down the heat and throw in the carrots. Gently simmer the soup until the carrots are cooked, about 15 minutes.

2 Add the pulses and spinach, and heat for a few minutes, stirring, until the spinach has wilted. Spoon in the pesto and gently mix into the soup. Serve with some crusty bread.

PER SERVING 219 kcals, protein 16g, carbs 34g, fat 3g, sat fat 3g, fibre 12g, sugar none, salt 3.16g

Chorizo & chickpea soup

For an Indian version of this spicy soup, use some cooked chicken and a teaspoon of curry paste instead of the chorizo.

 10 minutes 2

- 400g can chopped tomatoes
- 110g pack chorizo sausage (unsliced)
- 140g/5oz wedge Savoy cabbage
- sprinkling dried chilli flakes
- 410g can chickpeas, drained and rinsed
- 1 chicken or vegetable stock cube
- crusty or garlic bread, to serve

1 Put a medium pan on the heat and tip in the tomatoes followed by a canful of water. While the tomatoes are heating, quickly chop the chorizo into chunky pieces (removing any skin) and shred the cabbage.
2 Pile the chorizo and cabbage into the pan with the chilli flakes and chickpeas, then crumble in the stock cube. Stir well, cover and leave to bubble over a high heat for 6 minutes or until the cabbage is just tender. Ladle into bowls and eat with crusty or garlic bread.

PER SERVING 366 kcals, protein 23g, carbs 30g, fat 18g, sat fat 5g, fibre 9g, sugar trace, salt 4.26g

Smoked haddock chowder
. . . .

To give this simple, healthy soup a kick, add a dash of Tabasco sauce.

 20–25 minutes   2

- 1 onion, chopped
- 2 potatoes, scrubbed and sliced
- 500ml/18fl oz vegetable stock
- 2 smoked haddock fillets, about 100g/4oz each, cut into chunks
- 418g can creamed corn
- milk, to taste
- handful flat-leaf parsley, chopped (optional)

1 Put the onion and potatoes into a large pan. Pour over the vegetable stock and simmer for 6–8 minutes until the potatoes are soft, but still have a slight bite. Add the chunks of smoked haddock. Tip in the creamed corn and add a little milk if you like a thick chowder, more if you like it thinner.

2 Gently simmer the chowder for 5–7 minutes until the haddock is cooked (it should flake when prodded with a fork). Sprinkle over the parsley, if using, and ladle the chowder into bowls.

. . . .
PER SERVING 555 kcals, protein 37g, carbs 84g, fat 10g, sat fat 3g, fibre 7g, sugar none, salt 0.3g

Autumn-vegetable soup

A great soup for freezing ahead. Just reheat, make cheese on toast, if you like – it's very tasty with Edam – and serve.

 30–40 minutes 4

- 1 leek, chopped quite small
- 2 carrots, chopped quite small
- 1 potato, peeled and chopped quite small
- 1 garlic clove, finely chopped
- 1 tbsp finely chopped rosemary
- 425ml/¾ pint vegetable stock
- ½ tsp sugar
- 2 x 400g cans chopped tomatoes
- 410g can chickpeas, drained and rinsed
- 3 tbsp chopped flat-leaf parsley
- cheese on toast or buttered toast, to serve (optional)

1 Put the vegetables into a large pan with the garlic, rosemary, stock and sugar. Season and stir well, then bring to a simmer. Cover and cook gently for 15 minutes or until the vegetables are just tender.

2 Whizz the tomatoes in a food processor or with a hand blender until smooth, then tip into the vegetables with the chickpeas and parsley. Gently heat through, stirring now and then. Taste for seasoning and serve hot – with cheese on toast or buttered toast, if you like.

PER SERVING 151 kcals, protein 9g, carbs 25g, fat 2g, sat fat none, fibre 7g, sugar 1g, salt 1.14g

Thai chicken & coconut soup

For an even more authentic meal, serve this rich and creamy soup with some ready-cooked Thai fragrant rice.

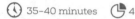 35–40 minutes 4

- 2 x 400g cans coconut milk
- 3 tbsp Thai fish sauce
- 4cm/1½in knob ginger or galangal, peeled and finely chopped
- 2 lemongrass stalks, finely sliced
- 6 kaffir lime leaves or strips of lime zest
- 1 red chilli, deseeded and chopped
- 2 tsp light muscovado sugar
- 500g/1lb 2oz boneless skinless chicken breasts, cut into small bite-sized pieces
- 2 tbsp lime juice
- good handful basil and coriander leaves, roughly chopped, to garnish

1 Tip all the ingredients except the chicken, lime juice and herbs into a large pan, bring to a gentle simmer and cook uncovered in a relaxed bubble for 5 minutes.
2 Add the chicken, cover and simmer for 8–10 minutes or until tender. Stir in the lime juice, then scatter over the herbs before serving.

PER SERVING 479 kcals, protein 35g, carbs 10g, fat 34g, sat fat 28g, fibre none, sugar 3g, salt 2.96g

Provençal tomato soup

Nothing compares with freshly made tomato soup. Wait until the autumn when tomatoes are at their tastiest.

 1½–1¾ hours 4

- 2 tbsp olive oil
- 1 onion, finely chopped
- 1 carrot, finely chopped
- 1 celery stick, finely chopped
- 2 tsp tomato purée, or to taste
- 1kg/2lb 4oz ripe tomatoes, quartered
- 2 bay leaves
- good pinch sugar, or to taste
- 1.2 litres/2 pints vegetable stock
- 4 tbsp crème fraîche, to dollop (optional)
- small handful basil leaves, to garnish (optional)

1 Heat the oil in a large pan and gently fry the onion, carrot and celery for 10 minutes until softened and lightly coloured. Stir in the tomato purée. Tip in the tomatoes and add the bay leaves and sugar. Season to taste. Stir well, cover and cook gently for 10 minutes until the tomatoes reduce down slightly.

2 Pour in the stock, stir and bring to the boil. Cover and cook gently for 30 minutes, stirring once or twice. Remove the bay leaves. Purée the soup in the pan with a hand blender until fairly smooth, then pour through a sieve to remove the tomato skins and seeds.

3 Return the soup to the pan and reheat. Taste and add more sugar, salt and pepper, if you like, plus some more tomato purée for a deeper colour. Serve hot, topped with crème fraîche and basil leaves, if you like.

PER SERVING 124 kcals, protein 4g, carbs 13g, fat 7g, sat fat 0.9g, fibre 4g, sugar 1g, salt 1.09g

Three green vegetable soup

The just wilted watercress and mint add a fresh and peppery flavour to this speedy, tasty soup.

 15 minutes 4

- knob butter or splash olive oil
- bunch spring onions, chopped
- 3 courgettes, chopped
- 200g/8oz podded fresh or frozen peas
- 850ml/1½ pints vegetable stock
- 85g bag trimmed watercress leaves
- large handful mint
- 2 rounded tbsp Greek yogurt, plus extra to drizzle

1 Heat the butter or oil in a large pan, add the spring onions and courgettes, and stir well. Cover and cook for 3 minutes, then add the peas and stock, and return to the boil. Cover and simmer for a further 4 minutes, then remove from the heat and stir in the watercress and mint until they are wilted.

2 Purée in the pan with a hand blender, adding the yogurt halfway through. Add some seasoning to taste. Serve hot or cold, drizzled with extra yogurt.

PER SERVING 100 kcals, protein 8g, carbs 9g, fat 4g, sat fat 2g, fibre 4g, sugar none, salt 0.81g

Cannellini bean soup

For a prepare-ahead dinner-party starter, freeze the soup at the end of stage 2 and reheat just before serving.

 1 hour 6

- 1 tbsp olive oil
- 4 shallots, finely chopped
- 2 garlic cloves, finely chopped
- 1 carrot, finely chopped
- 2 celery sticks, finely chopped
- 2 leeks, finely chopped
- 140g/5oz streaky bacon, finely chopped
- 1.4 litres/2½ pints chicken or vegetable stock
- 2 bay leaves
- 2 tsp chopped oregano or marjoram leaves or ½ tsp dried
- 2 x 425g cans cannellini beans, drained and rinsed
- handful flat-leaf parley, chopped
- extra virgin olive oil, to drizzle
- 6 tiny parsley sprigs, to garnish

1 Heat the oil in a large pan with a lid and tip in the shallots, garlic, carrot, celery, leeks and bacon. Cook over a medium heat for 5–7 minutes, stirring occasionally, until softened but not browned.

2 Pour in the stock, then add the bay leaves and oregano or marjoram. Season and bring to the boil, then cover the pan and simmer gently for 15 minutes. Tip in the beans, cover again and simmer for a further 5 minutes.

3 To serve, taste for seasoning and swirl in the chopped parsley. Ladle into warm bowls and top each with a drizzle of olive oil and a parsley sprig.

PER SERVING 214 kcals, protein 13g, carbs 19g, fat 10g, sat fat 3g, fibre 6g, sugar none, salt 1.78g

Chinese pork broth

This recipe uses pork tenderloin, which is a lean fillet that is good for braising, roasting or grilling whole and can also be sliced thinly for stir fries.

 20 minutes   4

- 400g/14oz pork tenderloin, cut into long thin strips
- 600ml/1 pint chicken stock
- 1 tbsp soy sauce
- 2 tsp Chinese five-spice powder
- large knob ginger, peeled and cut into matchsticks
- 200g pack baby leaf greens, quartered
- 1 red chilli, deseeded and finely chopped, or 1 tsp chilli flakes
- bunch spring onions, white and green parts sliced
- boiled rice or noodles, to serve

1 Tip all the ingredients, except the spring-onion green parts, into a large pan with a lid, cover and bring to a gentle simmer. Cook, without boiling, for about 8 minutes, until the pork has changed colour and the greens are cooked, but still a bit crunchy.
2 Ladle into bowls, scatter with the remaining spring onion and serve with boiled rice or noodles on the side.

PER SERVING 149 kcals, protein 24g, carbs 3g, fat 5g, sat fat 1g, fibre none, sugar 1g, salt 1.61g

Moroccan chickpea soup

An unusual and tasty dish for vegetarians. For meat-lovers, fry 4 sliced chorizo sausages along with the onions and celery.

 20–25 minutes 4

- 1 tbsp olive oil
- 1 medium onion, chopped
- 2 celery sticks, chopped
- 2 tsp ground cumin
- 600ml/1 pint vegetable stock
- 400g can chopped tomatoes with garlic
- 400g can chickpeas, drained and rinsed
- 100g/4oz frozen broad beans
- grated zest and juice ½ lemon
- large handful coriander or parsley, to garnish
- flatbread, to serve

1 Heat the oil in a large pan, then fry the onion and celery gently for 10 minutes until softened, stirring frequently. Tip in the cumin and fry for another minute.
2 Turn up the heat, then add the stock, tomatoes and chickpeas, plus a good grind of black pepper. Simmer for 8 minutes. Throw in the broad beans and lemon juice, and cook for a further 2 minutes.
3 Season to taste, then top with a sprinkling of lemon zest and the chopped herbs. Serve with flatbread.

PER SERVING 148 kcals, protein 9g, carbs 17g, fat 5g, sat fat 1g, fibre 6g, sugar none, salt 1.07g

White-bean soup with chilli oil

The perfect soup to start a Sunday lunch in winter. The chilli oil is the ideal foil to the mealiness of the beans.

 1½–1¾ hours, plus overnight soaking   6

- 500g/1lb 2oz dried butter beans, soaked overnight
- 2 tbsp vegetable oil
- 1 medium onion, chopped
- 1 garlic clove, chopped
- 2 carrots, chopped
- 2 celery sticks, chopped
- 1.4 litres/2½ pints vegetable stock
- 2 bay leaves
- 2–3 thyme sprigs, plus extra for sprinkling
- chilli oil, for drizzling

1 Drain the beans. Shuck off and discard the skins by pinching the beans between finger and thumb. Put the beans in a colander, rinse and drain.

2 Heat the oil in a pan, and fry the onion and garlic for 1–2 minutes. Tip in the carrots and celery, and fry gently for 2–3 minutes. Add the beans, stock, bay and thyme with some black pepper, and bring to the boil. Reduce the heat, then cover and simmer for 20–25 minutes, skimming off any scum, until the beans are soft.

3 Cool the soup for 10 minutes, discard the bay and thyme, then purée in the pan with a hand blender until quite smooth. Check for seasoning and reheat if necessary, then serve with a drizzle of chilli oil and a sprinkling of thyme leaves.

PER SERVING 319 kcals, protein 18g, carbs 49g, fat 7g, sat fat 1g, fibre 15g, sugar none, salt 0.89g

Roasted ratatouille chicken

A simple method and lovely Mediterranean flavours and colours make this a versatile dish, perfect for either a family supper or a dinner party.

 50 minutes–1 hour   4

- 1 onion, cut into wedges
- 2 red peppers, deseeded and cut into chunks
- 1 courgette (about 200g/8oz), cut into chunks
- 1 aubergine (about 300g/10oz), cut into chunks
- 4 tomatoes, halved
- 4 tbsp olive oil, plus extra for drizzling
- 4 chicken breasts, skin on (about 140g/5oz each)
- few rosemary sprigs (optional)

1 Heat oven to 200C/180C fan/gas 6. Lay all the vegetables and the tomatoes in a shallow roasting tin. Make sure they have lots of room – overcrowding will slow down the cooking. Pour over the olive oil and give the vegetables a good mix round until they are well coated (hands are easiest for this).

2 Nestle the chicken breasts on top of the vegetables and tuck in some rosemary sprigs, if you have them. Season everything with salt and black pepper, and drizzle a little oil over the chicken. Now roast for about 35 minutes until the vegetables are soft and the chicken is golden. Drizzle with more oil before serving.

PER SERVING 318 kcals, protein 37g, carbs 13g, fat 14g, sat fat 2g, fibre 4g, sugar none, salt 0.25g

Pork with orange, olives & bay

• •

This is great for cooking a day ahead and reheating. The flavours will become more intense, and the excess fat will be easy to lift off the top once the dish is cold.

 3¼ hours   6

- 85g/3oz sun-dried tomatoes in oil, roughly chopped, plus 2–3 tbsp oil from the jar
- 1kg/2lb 4oz pork shoulder, cut into chunky cubes
- 2 tbsp plain flour, seasoned
- 400g/14oz shallots
- 1 onion, thinly sliced
- 3 bay leaves
- few thyme sprigs
- 5 garlic cloves, thinly sliced
- 400ml/14fl oz red wine
- strip zest and juice 1 orange
- 350ml/12fl oz chicken stock
- 400g can chopped plum tomatoes
- 800g/1lb 12oz large new potatoes, halved or cut into fat slices, depending on size
- 70g pack pitted dry black olives

1 Heat 1 tablespoon of the tomato oil in a large flameproof casserole dish. Toss the pork in the seasoned flour, tap off any excess, then brown it in two batches, transferring to a large bowl once golden and crusted. Use a splash more oil for the second batch if needed.

2 Tip a further tablespoon of the oil, the shallots, onion, bay and thyme into the pan, and fry for 5 minutes until golden. Stir in the garlic and sun-dried tomatoes, cook for 1 minute more, then tip on to the pork.

3 Splash the wine and orange juice into the dish and boil hard for 5 minutes. Add the meat-and-onion mix back in.

4 Heat oven to 160C/140C fan/gas 3. Stir the stock, canned tomatoes, potatoes, olives and zest into the casserole, then bring to a simmer. Push the potatoes under the surface of the liquid. Cover, leaving a slight gap to one side, then cook in the oven for 2½ hours, or until the meat is tender enough to cut with a spoon. Spoon away any excess fat and let the stew rest for a few minutes before serving.

• •

PER SERVING 670 kcals, protein 37g, carbs 35g, fat 36g, sat fat 11g, fibre 7g, sugar 9g, salt 1.2g

Chicken with creamy bacon penne

This amazingly quick and tasty dish works well with fresh salmon, too. Just cook for 3 minutes on each side and leave out the bacon.

 10 minutes   2

- 1 tbsp olive oil
- 2 boneless skinless chicken breasts
- 100g/4oz smoked lardons
- 4 tbsp dry white wine
- 100g/4oz frozen petits pois
- 5 tbsp double cream
- 220g pack 'instant' cooked penne

1 Heat the oil in a deep non-stick frying pan, add the chicken breasts and scatter with the lardons. Leave to cook over a high heat for 4 minutes while you gather the other ingredients together.

2 Turn the chicken over in the pan, give the lardons a stir, then pour in the wine and let it bubble over a high heat until it has virtually evaporated. Now add the peas, cream and penne, then season and stir well. Cover the pan and cook for 4 minutes more until the chicken is cooked all the way through. Serve straight away.

PER SERVING 639 kcals, protein 48g, carbs 24g, fat 38g, sat fat 17g, fibre 3g, sugar none, salt 1.86g

Fruity lamb tagine

This satisfying and superhealthy one-pot takes a bit of time in the oven, but you can do something else while it cooks.

 1¾ hours, plus marinating 4

- 2 tbsp olive oil
- 500g/1lb 2oz lean diced lamb
- 1 large onion, roughly chopped
- 2 large carrots, quartered lengthways and cut into chunks
- 2 garlic cloves, finely chopped
- 2 tbsp ras-el-hanout spice mix
- 400g can chopped tomatoes
- 400g can chickpeas, drained and rinsed
- 200g/8oz dried apricots
- 600ml/1 pint chicken stock
- 120g pack pomegranate seeds, to garnish
- 2 large handfuls coriander leaves, roughly chopped, to scatter
- couscous or rice, to serve

1 Heat oven to 180C/160C fan/gas 4. Heat the oil in a casserole and brown the lamb on all sides. Scoop out on to a plate, then add the onion and carrots to the casserole, and cook for 2–3 minutes until golden. Add the garlic and cook for 1 minute more. Stir in the ras-el-hanout and tomatoes, and season. Tip the lamb back in with the chickpeas and apricots. Pour over the stock, stir and bring to a simmer. Cover the dish and put in the oven for 1 hour.

2 If the lamb is still a little tough, give it 20 minutes more until tender. When ready, leave it to rest so it's not piping hot, then serve scattered with pomegranate seeds and coriander, with couscous or rice alongside.

PER SERVING 497 kcals, protein 40g, carbs 46g, fat 18g, sat fat 5g, fibre 12g, sugar 32g, salt 1.3g

Home-style chicken curry

Go to a little extra effort and make your own curry paste for a really authentic Indian curry.

 45 minutes 4

- 1 large onion, roughly chopped
- 6 garlic cloves, roughly chopped
- 50g/2oz knob ginger, roughly chopped
- 4 tbsp vegetable oil
- 2 tsp cumin seeds
- 1 tsp fennel seeds
- 5cm/2in cinnamon stick
- 1 tsp chilli flakes
- 1 tsp garam masala
- 1 tsp turmeric powder
- 1 tsp caster sugar
- 400g can chopped tomatoes
- 8 skinless boneless chicken thighs (about 800g/1lb 12oz total), cut into 2.5cm/1in chunks
- 250ml/9fl oz hot chicken stock
- 2 tbsp chopped coriander leaves
- basmati rice and natural yogurt, to serve

1 Process the onion to a loose paste in a small food processor or with a hand blender with 3 tablespoons water. Then process the chopped garlic and ginger with 4 tablespoons water until smooth.

2 Heat the oil in a wok or heavy pan over a medium heat. Heat the cumin, fennel, cinnamon and chilli in the wok or pan for 30 seconds until the spices are aromatic. Add the onion paste then fry for 7–8 minutes or until the water evaporates and the onions turn dark golden. Add the garlic-and-ginger paste, and cook for 2 minutes, stirring.

3 Stir in the garam masala, turmeric and sugar, and cook for 20 seconds. Add the tomatoes. and cook on a medium heat for 10 minutes until the tomatoes reduce and darken.

4 Add the chicken to the wok or pan. Cook for 5 minutes then pour over the hot stock. Simmer for 8–10 minutes until the chicken is tender and the sauce lightly thickened.

5 Serve sprinkled with chopped coriander and basmati rice and a pot of yogurt on the side.

PER SERVING 382 kcals, protein 47g, carbs 11g, fat 178g, sat fat 3g, fibre 2g, sugar 7g, salt 0.8g

Sausage & leek hash

You can use any leftover vegetables for this simple weekend supper.

 30–35 minutes   4

- 2 tbsp olive oil
- 6 plump sausages
- 6 potatoes, thinly sliced
- 350g/12oz thinly sliced leeks (or broccoli or cabbage)
- 1 tbsp creamed horseradish sauce, or more to taste
- 100g/4oz mature Cheddar or Gruyère, grated

1 Heat half of the oil in a large heavy-based frying pan. Add the sausages and fry gently for 8–10 minutes until well browned. Remove the sausages, then slice them on the diagonal and set aside.

2 Turn the heat to medium and add the remaining oil to the pan. Add the potatoes and leeks (or broccoli/cabbage), and give everything a good stir. Cook until the potatoes and veg are tender and beginning to brown, turning them over from time to time. This will take 15–20 minutes.

3 Toss the sausages back in along with the horseradish, to taste, and heat through for a further 2–3 minutes. Take the pan off the heat, sprinkle in the cheese, season well and stir gently to combine. Serve.

PER SERVING 534 kcals, protein 24g, carbs 35g, fat 34g, sat fat 14g, fibre 4g, sugar trace, salt 2.46g

Chicken & thyme bake

· ·

Try Taleggio, ripe Brie, dolcelatte or Le Roulé, if you don't like goat's cheese.

 35–40 minutes   4

- 4 part-boned chicken breasts, skin on
- 140g/5oz firm goat's cheese, sliced
- bunch thyme
- 500g pack cherry tomatoes
- olive oil, for drizzling
- splash dry white wine
- French bread or ready-cooked saffron rice, to serve

1 Heat oven to 190C/170C fan/gas 5. Loosen the skin from the chicken breasts and stuff with the slices of goat's cheese and a thyme sprig. Put in a shallow ovenproof dish.

2 Halve the cherry tomatoes and scatter around the chicken with a few more thyme sprigs, a drizzle of olive oil and splash of white wine. Season with black pepper, and salt if you wish.

3 Bake for 25–30 minutes until the chicken is tender and golden. Serve with crusty French bread to mop up the juices or some saffron rice.

· ·

PER SERVING 330 kcals, protein 40g, carbs 5g, fat 16g, sat fat 8g, fibre 1g, sugar none, salt 1.24g

Pot-roast guinea fowl with lentils, sherry & bacon

· ·

This is one of those dishes that's easy to throw together but the end result has you brimming with pride. The herb-and-cream sauce is optional but delicious.

 1 hour 35 minutes   2-3

- 1 tbsp olive oil, plus extra for drizzling
- 50g/2oz butter
- 1 small guinea fowl
- 100g/4oz smoked bacon lardons
- 1 carrot, finely chopped
- 1 onion, finely chopped
- 2 celery sticks, finely chopped
- 2 bay leaves
- 100g/4oz Puy lentils
- 100ml/3½fl oz dry sherry
- 225ml/8fl oz chicken stock
- ½ bunch tarragon, leaves picked
- 1 tbsp Dijon mustard

FOR THE SAUCE
- 100ml/3½fl oz double cream
- juice ½ lemon
- handful each tarragon and parsley leaves

1 Heat oven to 180C/160C fan/gas 4. Heat the oil and butter in a flameproof casserole dish. Season the guinea fowl, gently fry on all sides for 10 minutes until browned, then remove to a plate.

2 Fry the bacon in the dish until starting to colour, then add the carrot, onion, celery and bay, and fry for 10 minutes until the veg have softened. Stir in the lentils, sherry and stock just to cover, and add the tarragon. Nestle the bird among the lentils, breast-side up, cover with a lid and roast for 1 hour.

3 Meanwhile, make the sauce. Bring the cream and lemon juice to the boil and season. Remove from the heat, add the herbs, purée with a hand blender and set aside.

4 Once cooked, remove the guinea fowl from the dish. Add the mustard and a drizzle of olive oil to the lentils, stir, then transfer them to a serving plate. Put the guinea fowl on top and serve with the sauce alongside.

· ·

PER SERVING (3) 796 kcals, protein 72g, carbs 23g, fat 40g, sat fat 16g, fibre 5g, sugar 7g, salt 2.4g

Chicken, ginger & green-bean hotpot

A light chicken casserole that makes a great Asian-inspired but chilli-free family meal that's ideal for kids and others who don't like spicy foods!

 35 minutes   2   Easily doubled

- ½ tbsp vegetable oil
- 2cm/¾in knob ginger, peeled and cut into matchsticks
- 1 garlic clove, chopped
- ½ onion, thinly sliced into half moons
- 1 tbsp Thai fish sauce
- ½ tbsp soft brown sugar
- 250g/9oz skinless boneless chicken thighs, trimmed of all fat and cut in half
- 125ml/4fl oz chicken stock
- 50g/2oz green beans, trimmed and cut into 2.5cm/1in lengths
- 1 tbsp chopped coriander leaves
- steamed rice, to serve

1 Heat the oil in a pan over a medium–high heat. Add the ginger, garlic and onion, and stir-fry for about 5 minutes or until lightly golden. Add the fish sauce, sugar, chicken and stock. Cover and cook over a medium heat for 15 minutes.
2 For the final 3 minutes of cooking, add the green beans. Remove from the heat and stir through half of the coriander. Serve with steamed rice and the remaining coriander scattered over.

PER SERVING 215 kcals, protein 30g, carbs 9g, fat 7g, sat fat 1g, fibre 2g, sugar 7g, salt 2g

Broccoli lemon chicken

Tenderstem broccoli is ideal for this dish as it cooks so quickly. Add a couple of minutes to the cooking time if you're using ordinary broccoli.

🕐 15–25 minutes   🍽 2 generously

- 1 tbsp groundnut or sunflower oil
- 340g pack mini chicken breast fillets (sometimes called goujons)
- 2 garlic cloves, sliced
- 200g pack Tenderstem broccoli, stems halved if very long
- 200ml/7fl oz chicken stock
- 1 heaped tsp cornflour
- 1 tbsp clear honey or 2 tsp golden caster sugar
- grated zest ½ lemon and juice 1 lemon
- large handful roasted cashew nuts

1 Heat the oil in a large frying pan or wok. Add the chicken and fry for 3–4 minutes until golden. Remove from the pan to a plate and add the garlic and broccoli. Stir-fry for a minute or so, then cover and cook for 2 minutes more, until almost tender.

2 Mix the stock, cornflour and honey or sugar well, then pour into the pan and stir until thickened. Tip the chicken back into the pan and let it heat through, then add the lemon zest and juice and the cashew nuts. Stir, then serve straight away.

PER SERVING 372 kcals, protein 48g, carbs 15g, fat 13g, sat fat 2g, fibre 3g, sugar 6g, salt 0.69g

Sunday brunch beans

Baked beans are great, cheap comfort food, and they're nutritious, too.

 20 minutes   2    Easily doubled

- 2 tbsp vegetable oil
- 1 potato, thinly sliced (unpeeled)
- 200g can corned beef, sliced
- 400g can baked beans
- splash Worcestershire sauce

1 Heat the oil in a frying pan until hot, add the potato slices and fry for 7–10 minutes or until golden and crisp.
2 Push the potatoes to one side, add the corned beef and fry undisturbed for a couple of minutes. Tip in the baked beans, add a splash of Worcestershire sauce and stir gently until the beans are hot and ready to serve.

PER SERVING 510 kcals, protein 37g, carbs 40g, fat 23g, sat fat 6g, fibre 8g, sugar 7g, salt 5g

Chicken biryani

. . . .

It's so easy to re-create this classic Indian dish that you'll never order a take-away again.

 1 hour   6

- 2 tbsp vegetable oil
- 6 large boneless chicken thighs, skin on
- 1 large onion, finely sliced
- 2 tbsp curry powder (hot, if you like it, mild for tamer curries)
- 350g/12oz easy-cook long grain rice
- 700ml/1¼ pints chicken or vegetable stock
- 250g/9oz frozen peas

1 Heat oven to 200C/180C fan/gas 6. Heat the oil in a large pan with a lid, and fry the chicken thighs, skin-side down, for 8–10 minutes until the skin is golden and crispy. Tip in the onion and continue to cook for 5 minutes until the onion softens. Sprinkle in the curry powder and cook for 1 minute more, then stir in the rice and pour over the stock. Bring the stock to the boil.

2 Cover the pan and bake for 30 minutes until all the liquid has been absorbed and the rice is cooked. Stir in the peas and leave the rice to stand for a few minutes before serving.

. . . .

PER SERVING 445 kcals, protein 32g, carbs 57g, fat 12g, sat fat 3g, fibre 2g, sugar none, salt 0.5g

Mediterranean vegetables with lamb

You get meat, vegetables and sauce from this clever one-pot, so all you need to serve with it is a hunk of crusty bread.

 45 minutes 4

- 1 tbsp olive oil
- 250g/9oz lean lamb fillet, trimmed of any fat and thinly sliced
- 140g/5oz shallots, halved
- 2 large courgettes, cut into chunks
- ½ tsp each ground cumin, paprika and ground coriander
- 1 red, 1 orange and 1 green pepper, deseeded and cut into chunks
- 1 garlic clove, sliced
- 150ml/¼ pint vegetable stock
- 250g/9oz cherry tomatoes
- handful coriander leaves, roughly chopped
- crusty bread, to serve (optional)

1 Heat the oil in a large heavy-based frying pan. Cook the lamb and shallots over a high heat for 2–3 minutes until golden. Add the courgettes and stir-fry for 3–4 minutes until beginning to soften.

2 Add the spices and toss well, then add the peppers and garlic. Reduce the heat and cook over a moderate heat for 4–5 minutes until they start to soften.

3 Pour in the stock and stir to coat. Add the tomatoes, season, then cover with a lid and simmer for 15 minutes, stirring occasionally until the veg are tender. Stir through the coriander to serve with some crusty bread, if you like.

PER SERVING 192 kcals, protein 17g, carbs 11g, fat 9g, sat fat 3g, fibre 4g, sugar 10g, salt 0.25g

Curry in a hurry

Look out for jars of ready-chopped ginger and chillies, and pouches of Gujarati masala in larger supermarkets.

 15 minutes 2  Easily doubled

- 1 tbsp sunflower oil
- 1 red onion, thinly sliced
- 1 garlic clove
- 2 tsp ready-prepared ginger from a jar
- ½–1 tsp ready-chopped chillies from a jar
- 200g can chopped tomatoes
- 250g/9oz boneless skinless chicken breasts, chopped
- 2 tsp Gujarati masala or garam masala
- 3 tbsp low-fat natural yogurt
- handful coriander leaves, roughly chopped
- warm garlic and coriander naan, to serve

1 Heat the oil in a pan, add the onion and fry until coloured. Crush the garlic into the pan, add the ginger and chillies, and cook briefly. Add the tomatoes and a quarter of a can of water, and bring to the boil. Simmer for 2 minutes, add the chicken and masala, then cover and cook for 5–6 minutes.

2 Reduce the heat to a simmer, then stir in the yogurt, a tablespoon at a time. Sprinkle with coriander and serve with warm garlic and coriander naans.

PER SERVING 252 kcals, protein 34g, carbs 11g, fat 8g, sat fat 1g, fibre 2g, sugar none, salt 0.46g

Bean & pasta stew with meatballs

Making meatballs out of sausages is a good weeknight short cut; because the sausage meat is already highly seasoned, all you need to do is roll it into balls.

 55 minutes   4

- 6–8 pack pork sausages
- 1 tbsp olive oil
- 2 onions, finely chopped
- 3 celery sticks, diced
- 2 carrots, diced
- 3 garlic cloves, finely chopped
- 400g can chopped tomatoes
- 1 litre/1¾ pints chicken stock
- 175g/6oz macaroni
- 410g can cannellini beans, drained and rinsed
- handful flat-leaf parsley leaves, chopped

1 Snip the ends off the sausages and squeeze out the meat. Roll into rough walnut-sized meatballs. Heat half the oil in a large wide pan and fry the sausage balls until browned, around 10 minutes. Remove from pan and set aside.

2 Add the rest of the oil to the pan. Tip in the onions, celery and carrots, and fry for 10 minutes until soft. Add the garlic and cook for 1 minute more. Tip in the tomatoes and stock. Bring to the boil and simmer for 10 minutes.

3 Stir in the macaroni and return the meatballs to the pan. Simmer for about 10 minutes until the pasta is cooked and the meatballs are cooked through. Stir in the beans and heat until piping hot. Season, mix in the parsley and serve.

PER SERVING 688 kcals, protein 34g, carbs 67g, fat 33g, sat fat 10g, fibre 10g, sugar 15g, salt 3.6g

Summer pork & potatoes

A great dish for everyone to help themselves from. A green salad, dressed lightly with olive oil and lemon juice, is all you need to go with it.

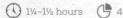 1¼–1½ hours 4

- olive oil, for drizzling
- 750g/1lb 10oz new potatoes, scrubbed and sliced
- 500g/1lb 2oz vine-ripened tomatoes, sliced
- 3–4 rosemary sprigs, leaves finely chopped
- 2 garlic cloves, chopped
- 4 pork chops or steaks
- dressed green salad, to serve

1 Heat oven to 200C/180C fan/gas 6. Drizzle a little olive oil over the base of a shallow ovenproof dish that is wide enough to take the chops or steaks in one layer. Arrange rows of potatoes and tomatoes across the dish, seasoning with salt and black pepper as you go and sprinkling with half the rosemary and all the garlic.

2 Drizzle a couple more tablespoons of the olive oil over the vegetables and bake for 30 minutes, then sit the pork on top, season and sprinkle with the remaining rosemary. Return to the oven for 35–45 minutes, until the pork and potatoes are tender. Serve with a dressed green salad.

PER SERVING 527 kcals, protein 25g, carbs 35g, fat 33g, sat fat 11g, fibre 3g, sugar none, salt 0.2g

Moroccan lemon chicken

Try using a whole preserved lemon from a jar instead of half a fresh lemon.

 40–45 minutes 4

- 1kg pack boneless skinless chicken thighs
- 1 onion, chopped
- 3 garlic cloves, crushed
- 1 tbsp pilau rice seasoning
- 2 tbsp olive oil
- ½ lemon, finely chopped – the zest, pith and flesh
- 100g pack whole blanched almonds
- 140g/5oz green olives (the ones with stones in taste best)
- 250ml/9fl oz chicken stock
- large handful coriander or flat-leaf parsley leaves, chopped

1 Toss the chicken with the onion, garlic, rice seasoning and oil in a microwave dish. Microwave on High for 8 minutes until everything is beginning to sizzle and the chicken is starting to change colour.
2 Toss the lemon, almonds and olives over the chicken. Pour in the stock and stir, keeping the chicken in a single layer.
3 Cover the dish with cling film, pierce a few times to allow the steam to escape, then return to the microwave on High for another 20 minutes until the liquid is bubbling vigorously and the chicken is cooked. Leave to stand for a few minutes before stirring in the coriander or parsley, then serve.

PER SERVING 488 kcals, protein 49g, carbs 8g, fat 29g, sat fat 5g, fibre 3g, sugar none, salt 2.68g

Frying-pan sausage hotpot

Ready-sliced, cooked long-life potatoes make this a really speedy supper dish.

 25–35 minutes 3

- 1 tbsp vegetable oil
- 6 plump good-quality sausages with herbs
- splash red wine (optional)
- 175ml/6fl oz vegetable stock
- 3 tbsp ready-prepared caramelised red onions
- 400g pack cooked sliced long-life potatoes

1 Heat the oil in a medium frying pan (one in which the sausages will fit fairly snugly). Add the sausages and fry for 8–10 minutes, turning them often. Heat grill to high. Splash a couple of tablespoons of red wine, if using, into the pan, then pour in the stock and stir in the caramelised red onions. Allow the mixture to bubble for 3–4 minutes, so it thickens a little and turns into a rich gravy. Remove from the heat.

2 Spread the potatoes so they roughly cover the sausages and gravy. Put the frying pan under the grill for about 8 minutes until the potatoes turn crisp and golden. Serve while bubbling and hot – there is no need to add seasoning.

PER SERVING 578 kcals, protein 20g, carbs 36g, fat 40g, sat fat 14g, fibre 4g, sugar 1g, salt 5.07g

Turkish lamb pilau

Fantastic textures and wonderful smells make this a very popular dish. You can use chicken and chicken stock, if you prefer.

 25–30 minutes   4

- small handful pine nuts or flaked almonds
- 1 tbsp olive oil
- 1 large onion, halved and sliced
- 2 cinnamon sticks, broken in half
- 500g/1lb 2oz lean fillet or leg of lamb, cubed
- 250g/9oz basmati rice
- 1 lamb or vegetable stock cube
- 12 ready-to-eat dried apricots
- handful mint leaves, roughly chopped

1 Dry-fry the pine nuts or almonds in a large pan until lightly toasted, then tip on to a plate. Add the oil to the pan, then fry the onion and cinnamon together until starting to turn golden. Turn up the heat, stir in the lamb, fry until the meat changes colour, then tip in the rice and cook for 1 minute, stirring all the time.

2 Pour in 500ml/18fl oz boiling water, crumble in the stock cube, add the apricots, then season to taste. Turn the heat down, cover and simmer for 12 minutes until the rice is tender and the stock has been absorbed. Toss in the pine nuts or almonds and mint, and serve.

PER SERVING 584 kcals, protein 32g, carbs 65g, fat 24g, sat fat 9g, fibre 3g, sugar none, salt 1.4g

Spring-chicken paella

Throw a new spin on the classic Spanish-rice one-pot by adding broad beans and some dill, mint and parsley for extra flavour.

 1¼ hours  4–5

- 6 chicken thighs, skin on
- 2 tbsp plain flour
- 3 tbsp olive oil
- 2 onions, finely chopped
- 3 garlic cloves, finely sliced
- 400g/14oz paella rice
- 1 tsp sweet paprika
- 2 good pinches saffron
- zest and juice 2 lemons
- 1.5 litres/2¾ pints chicken stock
- 200g/8oz each fresh or frozen peas and broad beans (weight after podding and skinning)
- ½ small bunch each dill, mint and parsley leaves, chopped

1 Heat oven to 180C/160C fan/gas 4. Season the chicken thighs well and then dust all over with the flour. Heat 1 tablespoon of the oil in a paella pan or large, deep frying pan. Fry the thighs until golden brown all over, then transfer to a shallow roasting tin and finish in the oven, cooking for 30–40 minutes.

2 Add the remaining oil, onions and garlic to the pan, and fry very gently until soft, 10–15 minutes. Stir in the rice, paprika, saffron and lemon zest, then add the stock and simmer, stirring occasionally, for about 20 minutes on a medium heat until the rice is nearly cooked.

3 Add the peas, broad beans and juice of 1 of the lemons and continue to cook until the rice and veg are just cooked through. Stir through the herbs and as much of the remaining lemon juice as it needs, along with some seasoning. Tuck the chicken thighs back in and cover for 5 minutes to let everything settle before serving.

PER SERVING (5) 660 kcals, protein 41g, carbs 79g, fat 20g, sat fat 5g, fibre 10g, sugar 5g, salt 1g

Spiced pork with stir-fried greens

Use a proper stir-fry oil, if you can, as it's infused with ginger, garlic and spices, giving a real flavour hit.

 20 minutes 2  Easily doubled

- 1 tbsp stir-fry or vegetable oil
- 250g/9oz pork escalopes, sliced into thin strips
- bunch spring onions, trimmed and sliced
- 175g/6oz broccoli, broken into small bite-sized florets
- 3 celery sticks, sliced
- 2 heads pak choi, broken into separate leaves
- 2 tbsp chopped coriander leaves
- finely grated zest and juice 1 lime
- a few thin slices red chilli or a dash sweet chilli sauce

1 Heat the oil in a wok or large frying pan, add the pork and stir-fry briskly for 3–4 minutes. Tip in the spring onions, broccoli and celery, and stir-fry over a high heat for 4 more minutes.
2 Add the pak choi and cook for a minute or so until the leaves have wilted. Toss in the coriander and lime zest, squeeze in a little lime juice and add the chilli slices or sauce. Season with salt and pepper, and serve straight away.

PER SERVING 260 kcals, protein 34g, carbs 5g, fat 12g, sat fat 2g, fibre 4g, sugar none, salt 0.59g

Spicy sausages & beans

This comforting sausage casserole is budget friendly and on the table in less than 30 minutes, making it perfect for a weeknight before payday.

 25 minutes   4

- 1 tbsp vegetable oil
- 1 onion, thickly sliced
- 8 Cumberland sausages
- 1 fat garlic clove, crushed
- 2 x 400g cans kidney beans in chilli sauce
- 2–3 curly parsley sprigs, chopped, to garnish

1 Heat the oil in a large frying pan. Cook the onion and sausages over a fairly high heat for 8–10 minutes, turning the sausages often so they brown all over.

2 Add the garlic to the pan with the kidney beans and their sauce. Half-fill one of the cans with water, swirl and then add this to the pan. Stir everything together and bring to the boil. Turn down to simmer and cook for 10 minutes, or until the sausages are cooked through. Season and sprinkle with the parsley, to serve.

PER SERVING 524 kcals, protein 24g, carbs 41g, fat 29g, sat fat 10g, fibre 11g, sugar 15g, salt 3.6g

Chicken & spring-vegetable stew

A fresh and delicious dish that's good enough to eat every day.

 25–30 minutes 2

- 2 boneless chicken breasts, skin on
- 1 tbsp olive oil
- 200g/8oz baby new potatoes, scrubbed and thinly sliced
- 500ml/18fl oz chicken stock
- 200g pack mixed spring vegetables (broccoli, peas, broad beans and sliced courgette)
- 2 tbsp crème fraîche
- handful tarragon leaves, roughly chopped, or ½ tsp dried tarragon

1 Fry the chicken in the olive oil in a wide pan with a lid for 5 minutes on each side. Throw in the potatoes and stir to coat. Pour over the chicken stock, cover and simmer for 10 minutes until the potatoes are almost cooked through.
2 Remove the lid and turn the heat to high. Boil the stock down until it just coats the bottom of the pan. Scatter the vegetables into the pan, cover again and cook for about 3 minutes.
3 Stir in the crème fraîche to make a creamy sauce, season with salt and pepper to taste, then add the tarragon. Serve straight from the pan.

PER SERVING 386 kcals, protein 38g, carbs 23g, fat 16g, sat fat 6g, fibre 3g, sugar none, salt 1.5g

Cheesy chops & chips

Get your protein hit with this all-in-one roast.

🕐 1–1¼ hours　　🍴 4

- 1kg/2lb 4oz potatoes, peeled and thickly sliced
- 1 onion, thinly sliced
- splash cider, wine, water or stock
- 2 tbsp olive oil
- 4 pork chops, about 175g/6oz each
- 100g/4oz Cheddar, grated
- 1 tbsp wholegrain mustard
- 3 tbsp milk

1 Heat oven to 230C/210C fan/gas 8. Toss the potatoes, onion, liquid and oil together in a large flameproof casserole. Season, if you like, then bake for 20–30 minutes until the potatoes start to brown. Lay the chops on the potatoes and cook for 10 minutes more.

2 Mix the cheese, mustard and milk together. When the chops have had 10 minutes in the oven, spread the cheese mixture over them and switch the oven over to high grill. Put the pan under the grill and cook for about 5 minutes until the cheese is bubbling and the potatoes are golden and crispy. Serve straight from the pan.

PER SERVING 580 kcals, protein 42g, carbs 40g, fat 32g, sat fat 14g, fibre 5g, sugar none, salt 1.6g

Pizza-chicken melts

With only five ingredients, this is a great after-work meal.

 10–15 minutes   2  Easily halved or doubled

- 2 small boneless skinless chicken breasts
- 1 tbsp olive oil
- 50g/2oz Cheddar, grated
- 4 cherry tomatoes, quartered
- 2 tsp pesto sauce
- green salad, to serve

1 Heat grill to high. Sandwich the chicken between cling film or two plastic food bags and beat firmly with a rolling pin or the bottom of a pan to flatten. Heat the oil in a non-stick frying pan, add the chicken and cook for 2 minutes on each side until golden.

2 While the chicken cooks, mix the cheese and tomatoes together. Take the chicken from the pan and wipe out the oil with kitchen paper. Return the chicken to the pan, spread each breast with a teaspoon of pesto, then pile the cheese and tomatoes on top.

3 Put the pan under the hot grill for a minute or so (protect the handle with foil, if you think it is likely to burn), until the cheese has melted. Serve with a green salad.

PER SERVING 315 kcals, protein 37g, carbs 1g, fat 18g, sat fat 8g, fibre none, sugar none, salt 0.68g

Oven-baked leek & bacon risotto

Cooking a risotto in the oven saves you the effort of standing over the pan stirring continuously – and the final result is just as creamy.

 40 minutes 4

- 1 tbsp olive oil
- 6 rashers smoked back bacon, roughly chopped
- 2 leeks, halved lengthways and finely sliced
- 250g/9oz risotto rice
- 700ml/1¼ pints hot chicken or vegetable stock
- 175g/6oz frozen peas
- 3 tbsp soft cheese
- zest 1 lemon

1 Heat oven to 200C/180C fan/gas 6. Heat the oil in an ovenproof shallow pan with a lid. Add the bacon and fry for 2 minutes. Add the leeks and cook until soft, but not coloured, 4–5 minutes. Tip in the rice and cook for 1 minute more, then pour over the stock. Cover and put in the oven for 20 minutes, stirring halfway through the cooking time.

2 When the rice is just tender and all the liquid has been absorbed, remove from the oven and stir in the peas. Return to the oven for 2 minutes more. Remove the risotto from the oven and stir through the cheese. Add the lemon zest and season to serve straight away.

PER SERVING 424 kcals, protein 22g, carbs 55g, fat 14g, sat fat 5g, fibre 5g, sugar 3g, salt 2.34g

Spicy chicken & bean stew

If you have any leftovers from this dish, shred the chicken, then stir it back into the sauce to make a burrito or taco filling..

 1 hour 35 minutes 6

- about 1.25kg/2lb 12oz chicken thighs and drumsticks
- 1 tbsp olive oil
- 2 onions, sliced
- 1 garlic clove, crushed
- 2 red chillies, deseeded and chopped
- 250g/9oz frozen sliced peppers, defrosted
- 400g can chopped tomatoes
- 420g can kidney beans in chilli sauce
- 2 x 400g cans butter beans, drained and rinsed
- 400ml/14fl oz hot chicken stock
- small bunch coriander, chopped
- soured cream and crusty bread, to serve

1 Pull the skin off the chicken and discard. Heat the oil in a large casserole dish, brown the chicken all over, then remove with a slotted spoon to a plate. Tip in the onions, garlic and chillies, then fry for 5 minutes until starting to soften and turn golden.

2 Add the peppers, tomatoes, kidney beans with their sauce, butter beans and hot stock. Put the chicken back on top, half-cover with the casserole lid and cook for 50 minutes, until the chicken is cooked through and tender.

3 Stir through the coriander and serve with soured cream and crusty bread.

PER SERVING 366 kcals, protein 38g, carbs 30g, fat 11g, sat fat 5g, fibre 9g, sugar 12g, salt 2.45g

Oven-baked risotto

Cook this simple storecupboard risotto in the oven while you get on with something else – the result is still wonderfully creamy.

 30–35 minutes   4

- 250g pack smoked bacon, chopped into small pieces
- 1 onion, chopped
- 25g/1oz butter
- 300g/10oz risotto rice
- half a glass white wine (optional)
- 150g pack cherry tomatoes, halved
- 700ml/1¼ pint hot chicken stock (from a cube is fine)
- 50g/2oz Parmesan, grated

1 Heat oven to 200C/180C fan/gas 6. Fry the bacon pieces in an ovenproof pan or casserole dish with a lid for 3–5 minutes until golden and crisp. Stir in the onion and butter, and cook for 3–4 minutes until soft. Tip in the rice and mix well until coated. Pour over the wine, if using, and cook for 2 minutes until absorbed.
2 Add the cherry tomatoes and the hot stock, then give the rice a quick stir. Cover with a tightly fitting lid and bake for 18 minutes until just cooked.
3 Stir through most of the Parmesan and serve sprinkled with the remainder.

PER SERVING 517 kcals, protein 22g, carbs 63g, fat 20g, sat fat 10g, fibre 2g, sugar none, salt 3.38g

Haddock in tomato-basil sauce

. . . .

One-pot dishes are often healthy as well as simple. This easy fish recipe proves that reducing fat doesn't mean reducing flavour.

 40–50 minutes   4

- 1 tbsp olive oil
- 1 onion, thinly sliced
- 1 small aubergine, about 250g/9oz, roughly chopped
- ½ tsp paprika
- 2 garlic cloves, crushed
- 400g can chopped tomatoes
- 1 tsp dark or light muscovado sugar
- 8 large basil leaves, plus a few extra, to garnish
- 4 x 175g/6oz firm skinless white fish fillets, such as haddock
- salad and crusty bread, to serve

1 Heat the oil in a large non-stick frying pan with a lid and stir-fry the onion and aubergine for about 4 minutes until they start to turn golden. Cover with a lid and let the vegetables steam-fry in their own juices for 6 minutes – this helps them to soften without needing any extra oil.

2 Stir in the paprika, garlic, tomatoes and sugar with ½ teaspoon salt and cook for 8–10 minutes, stirring often, until the vegetables are tender.

3 Scatter in the basil leaves, then nestle the fish in the sauce. Cover and cook for 6–8 minutes until the fish flakes easily when tested with a fork. Tear over the rest of the basil and serve with a salad and crusty bread.

. . . .

PER SERVING 212 kcals, protein 36g, carbs 8g, fat 4g, sat fat 1g, fibre 3g, sugar 1g, salt 0.5g

Fish o'leekie

Accurate microwave timings ensure that everything is cooked together perfectly.

 20–25 minutes 4

- 1 leek, finely sliced
- 100g/4oz lean smoked back bacon, chopped
- 500ml/18fl oz vegetable stock
- 300g/10oz American easy-cook rice
- 500g/1lb 2oz cod or haddock fillet, skinned and cut into large chunks
- 3 tbsp chopped parsley leaves
- grated zest and juice 1 lemon

1 Put the leek and bacon in a medium microwave dish with 4 tablespoons of the stock. Cover the dish with cling film, pierce the film with a knife and microwave on High for 5 minutes.
2 Uncover the dish and stir the rice and remaining stock into the leek and bacon. Microwave on High for a further 5 minutes.
3 Gently stir in the fish chunks, cover the dish with cling film again, pierce the film with a knife and cook for a further 10 minutes until the fish and rice are done.
4 Stir in the parsley and lemon zest and juice. Leave to stand for 2–3 minutes before serving.

PER SERVING 437 kcals, protein 35g, carbs 66g, fat 6g, sat fat 1g, fibre 1g, sugar none, salt 1.8g

Prawn pilau

You can use cooked, chopped chicken instead of the prawns, if you prefer.

 25–30 minutes 4

- 2 tbsp korma curry paste
- 1 small onion, finely chopped
- 300g/10oz basmati rice, drained and rinsed
- 700ml/1¼ pints chicken stock
- 150g pack cooked peeled prawns, defrosted if frozen
- cupful frozen peas
- 1 red chilli, deseeded and sliced into rings
- handful coriander leaves, chopped
- lemon wedges, to squeeze over

1 Heat a large wide pan and dry-fry the curry paste with the onion for 4–5 minutes until the onion begins to soften. Add the rice to the pan and stir to coat in the curry paste. Add the stock, then bring to the boil.

2 Cover the pan and turn the heat down to low. Leave the rice to simmer slowly for 12–15 minutes until the liquid has been absorbed and the rice is cooked. Turn off the heat and stir in the prawns, peas and chilli. Cover the pan and leave to stand for 5 minutes.

3 Fluff up the rice grains with a fork and season, if you want. Scatter over the coriander and serve with lemon wedges.

PER SERVING 340 kcals, protein 18g, carbs 65g, fat 3g, sat fat 1g, fibre 2g, sugar none, salt 2.38g

Sea bass & seafood Italian stew

Just plonk this dish in the middle of the table, lift off the lid and your guests will realise that impressive food doesn't have to be fussy or fancy.

 1 hour 4

- 2 tbsp olive oil
- 1 fennel bulb, halved and sliced, fronds kept separate to garnish
- 2 garlic cloves, sliced
- ½ red chilli, deseeded and chopped
- 250g/9oz squid, cleaned and sliced into rings
- bunch basil, leaves and stalks separated, stalks tied together, leaves roughly chopped
- 400g can chopped tomatoes
- 150ml/¼ pint white wine
- 2 large handfuls mussels or clams
- 8 large raw prawns (whole look nicest), shell on
- 4 sea bass fillets (about 140g/5oz each)
- crusty bread, to serve

1 Heat the oil in a large pan with a tight-fitting lid, then add the sliced fennel, garlic and chilli. Fry until softened, then add the squid, basil stalks, tomatoes and wine. Simmer over a low heat for 35 minutes until the squid is tender and the sauce has thickened slightly, then season.

2 Scatter the mussels or clams and prawns over the sauce, lay the sea bass fillets on top, cover, turn up the heat and cook on high for 5 minutes. Scatter with the basil leaves and fennel fronds, and serve with some crusty bread.

PER SERVING 329 kcals, protein 45g, carbs 7g, fat 11g, sat fat 2g, fibre 2g, sugar 4g, salt 1g

Chilli prawn noodles

A light and aromatic dish made entirely from storecupboard ingredients.

 30–40 minutes   4

- 2 tbsp olive oil
- 1 onion, roughly chopped
- 1 heaped tbsp coriander purée (from a tube)
- pinch dried chilli flakes, or to taste
- 400g can chopped tomatoes with garlic
- 1 heaped tbsp tomato purée
- 1 tbsp vegetable bouillon powder
- 150g pack straight-to-wok noodles
- 400g/14oz frozen cooked and peeled prawns (large North Atlantic ones are tender and juicy)
- sugar (optional)

1 Heat the oil in a wok or deep frying pan. Toss in the onion, squeeze in the coriander purée and sprinkle over the chilli flakes to taste (go easy at this stage). Stir-fry for 5 minutes until the onion is softened but not browned.

2 Pour in the tomatoes and 1½ canfuls hot water, add the tomato purée and sprinkle over the bouillon powder. Season well. Bring to a bubble, stirring, then lower the heat and let the sauce simmer gently for about 15 minutes until slightly reduced but still runny.

3 When the sauce is ready, tip in the noodles and frozen prawns. Stir well and heat through for 2 minutes only – just to defrost the prawns and heat through the noodles. Taste for seasoning before serving, and add more chilli flakes and a little sugar if you like.

PER SERVING 228 kcals, protein 22g, carbs 18g, fat 8g, sat fat 1g, fibre 2g, sugar none, salt 2.95g

Spiced-bulghar pilaf with fish

Ring the changes by using healthy bulghar wheat in a pilaf instead of rice and choosing a sustainable white fish like pollack instead of cod.

 45 minutes   4

- 1 tbsp olive oil
- 2 onions, finely sliced
- 3 carrots, grated
- 2 tsp cumin seeds
- 2 tbsp harissa paste
- 200g/8oz bulghar wheat
- 6 dried apricots, chopped
- 700ml/1¼ pints weak chicken stock (we used 1 stock cube)
- 200g/8oz baby leaf spinach
- 4 firm skinless white fish fillets
- 4 thin lemon slices

1 Heat the oil in a lidded flameproof casserole dish. Tip in the onions and cook for 10 minutes until soft and golden. Add the carrots and cumin seeds, and cook for 2 minutes more. Stir through the harissa, bulghar and apricots, pour over the stock and bring to the boil. Cover and simmer for 7 minutes.

2 Add the spinach and stir through until just wilted. Arrange the fish fillets on top, pop a slice of lemon on each and season. Replace the lid and cook for 8 minutes, keeping over a low-ish heat.

3 Turn heat to low and cook for 7–8 minutes more or until the fish is cooked through and the bulghar is tender. Season with black pepper and serve.

PER SERVING 416 kcals, protein 37g, carbs 52g, fat 6g, sat fat 1g, fibre 7g, sugar 15g, salt 1g

Fragrant courgette & prawn curry

Wondering what to do with a glut of courgettes? Put them to good use in this spicy, summery one-pot.

 35 minutes   2

- 2 tbsp sunflower oil
- 500g/1lb 2oz courgettes, thickly sliced
- ½ tsp cumin seeds
- 2 tbsp finely chopped ginger
- 6 garlic cloves, crushed
- 1 red chilli, deseeded and finely chopped
- 1 tsp ground coriander
- ¼ tsp ground turmeric
- 500g/1lb 2oz tomatoes, chopped
- 150ml/¼ pint hot vegetable stock
- 225g pack raw peeled frozen jumbo prawns, thawed
- ½ small bunch coriander, roughly chopped
- basmati rice and mango chutney, to serve (optional)

1 Heat the oil in a large wok and stir-fry the courgettes for 5–6 minutes until softened. Lift from the wok to a plate with a slotted spoon, leaving the oil behind. Set aside.

2 Add the cumin seeds to the wok and toast for a few seconds, then add the ginger, garlic, chilli and spices. Cook, stirring, for 1–2 minutes, then tip in the tomatoes and cook for a few minutes more.

3 Pour in the stock and simmer to make a pulpy sauce, then add the courgettes and prawns. Cook gently until the prawns change from grey to pink and the courgettes are tender but not too soft. Stir in most of the coriander, saving some to sprinkle over the top.

4 Serve with basmati rice and mango chutney, if you like, and scatter over the remaining coriander.

. . . .
PER SERVING 305 kcals, protein 28g, carbs 17g, fat 15g, sat fat 2g, fibre 5g, sugar 13g, salt 1.41g

Chorizo, new potatoes & haddock

. . . .

This simple way to cook fish delivers a fantastic result with minimum effort. If you don't have dry sherry to cook with, a good white wine will do just as well.

 30 minutes   2

- 1 tbsp extra virgin olive oil, plus extra to drizzle
- 50g/2oz chorizo, peeled and thinly sliced
- 450g/1lb salad or new potatoes, sliced
- 4 tbsp dry sherry, or more if you need it
- 2 skinless thick fillets white fish (such as sustainably caught haddock)
- good handful cherry tomatoes, halved
- 20g bunch flat-leaf parsley, chopped
- crusty bread, to serve

1 Heat a large lidded frying pan, then add the oil. Tip in the chorizo, fry for 2 minutes until it starts to release its oils, then tip in the potatoes and some seasoning. Splash over 3 tablespoons of the sherry, cover the pan tightly, then leave to cook for 10–15 minutes until the potatoes are just tender. Move them around the pan a bit halfway through.

2 Season the fish well. Give the potatoes another stir, add the cherry tomatoes and most of the chopped parsley to the pan, then lay the fish on top. Splash over 1 tablespoon more of the sherry, put the lid on again, then leave to cook for 5 minutes, or until the fish has turned white and is flaky when prodded in the middle. Scatter the whole dish with the rest of the parsley and drizzle with more olive oil. Serve straight away with crusty bread.

. . . .
PER SERVING 534 kcals, protein 47g, carbs 39g, fat 19g, sat fat 4g, fibre 3g, sugar 5g, salt 0.79g

Fish with lemon & beans

This is a speedy supper dish that gives you a great sense of well-being. Try stirring in capers, olives or peppers for a slightly different taste.

 10 minutes ⏲ 2

- 400g can butter beans, drained and rinsed
- 3 tbsp lemon-infused olive oil or olive oil mixed with a little lemon juice
- 2 handfuls parsley leaves, roughly chopped
- 100g/4oz piece chorizo sausage, skinned and chopped into small chunks
- 2 x 175g/6oz skinless white fish fillets, such as cod

1 Tip the butter beans into a shallow microwave dish. Stir in half the lemon oil, half the parsley and all the chorizo. Top with the fish fillets and the remaining oil. Cover the dish with cling film and pierce a few times. Microwave on High for 4–5 minutes, until the fish looks opaque and flakes easily.

2 Remove the fish from the dish. Stir the beans and chorizo together and spoon on to plates. Top with the fish and scatter with the remaining parsley.

PER SERVING 523 kcals, protein 48g, carbs 17g, fat 30g, sat fat 7g, fibre 6g, sugar none, salt 2g

Squid & pinto bean stew

We tend to think of squid as something that's cooked quickly but it also lends itself to slow cooking, which makes it very tender.

 1½ hours   4

- 2 tbsp olive oil
- 1 onion, finely chopped
- 4 carrots, peeled, 1 left whole, 3 cut into rounds
- 2 celery sticks, diced
- 3 garlic cloves, finely chopped
- 800g/1lb 12oz prepared squid cut into rings, the tentacles left whole
- 1 tbsp tomato purée
- 1 thyme sprig
- 680g jar passata
- 500g pot fresh chicken stock
- 400g tin pinto beans, drained and rinsed
- chopped parsley, to garnish
- wilted greens, to serve (optional)

1 Heat a flameproof casserole dish with 2 tablespoons oil. Toss in the onion, carrot, celery and the chopped garlic. Fry gently for 15 minutes until the vegetables are tender. Stir through the squid, tomato purée and thyme sprig. Cook for a minute or two, then pour over the passata and chicken stock. Bring to the boil, turn down the heat, pop on the lid and simmer for 45 minutes, stirring occasionally. Take off the lid and cook down for 30 minutes.

2 Heat oven to 220C/200C fan/gas 7. Stir in the beans. Cook until the squid is totally tender and the sauce has thickened.

3 Scatter parsley over the stew and serve with some wilted greens, if you like.

PER SERVING 401 kcals, protein 42g, carbs 31g, fat 10g, sat fat 2g, fibre 7g, sugar 17g, salt 1.4g

Smoked salmon & celeriac bake

This is a Swedish-inspired, rich supper dish using easily available ingredients.

 2 hours 6

- juice 1 lemon
- 1 small celeriac, about 650g/1lb 7oz
- 2 medium baking potatoes
- 2 x 125g packs sliced smoked salmon
- small handful dill, chopped
- 1 onion, finely sliced
- 284ml pot double cream

1 Heat oven to 200C/180C fan/gas 6. Pour the lemon juice into a large bowl. Peel and quarter the celeriac, cut into slices the thickness of a £1 coin and toss into the lemon juice. Peel and thinly slice the potatoes and toss with the celeriac.

2 Layer the celeriac, potatoes and salmon slices in a large ovenproof dish, sprinkling dill, onion and cream over each layer, together with a little salt and plenty of black pepper. You should have three layers of vegetables with two layers of salmon, onion and dill. Finish with the remaining cream.

3 Cover the dish with foil, put on a baking sheet and bake for 45 minutes. Uncover and bake for 30–40 minutes more, until the vegetables feel tender when pierced and the top is golden. Cool slightly before serving.

PER SERVING 328 kcals, protein 14g, carbs 13g, fat 25g, sat fat 15g, fibre 3g, sugar none, salt 2.19g

Thai-prawn fried rice

This delicious Asian supper is faster, healthier and cheaper than a take-away – ready in a superquick 20 minutes.

 20 minutes 2

- 1 tbsp sunflower oil
- 1 red pepper, deseeded, quartered and cut into diagonal strips
- 5 spring onions, whites roughly chopped, greens finely chopped
- 100g/4oz broccoli, cut into small florets
- 2 tbsp Thai green curry paste
- 200g pack raw and peeled king prawns, thawed if frozen
- 250g pack pre-steamed coconut basmati rice
- 100g/4oz frozen peas
- 100g/4oz beansprouts
- handful torn basil leaves
- Thai fish sauce, to taste

1 Heat the oil in a wok and stir-fry the pepper, whites of the onions and broccoli for a few minutes to soften. Stir in the curry paste and prawns, and cook for 1 minute more.
2 Add a splash of water, then crumble in the coconut rice, breaking it up with a spoon. Tip in the peas, beansprouts and greens of the onions, and stir-fry until everything has heated through, then add the basil and fish sauce to taste.

PER SERVING 457 kcals, protein 33g, carbs 42g, fat 17g, sat fat 5g, fibre 11g, sugar 10g, salt 1.8g

Italian-style roasted fish

Let the fresh flavours of the Mediterranean into your home with this delicious one-pot dish.

🕐 25–30 minutes 🥧 4

- 4 thick firm white fish fillets, such as cod, haddock, hoki or pollack, skin on
- 1 tbsp olive oil, plus extra for drizzling
- 500g/1lb 2oz cherry tomatoes, halved
- 50g/2oz pitted black olives, halved
- 25g/1oz pine nuts
- large handful basil leaves

1 Heat oven to 200C/180C fan/gas 6. Season the fish. Heat the oil in a large roasting tin on top of the stove and cook the fillets, skin-side down, for 2–3 minutes or until just crisp.
2 Scatter the tomatoes, olives and pine nuts around the fish, season and roast in the oven for 12–15 minutes until the fish flakes easily with a fork. Scatter with the basil leaves and drizzle with a little olive oil before serving.

PER SERVING 242 kcals, protein 30g, carbs 4g, fat 12g, sat fat 2g, fibre 2g, sugar none, salt 0.99g

Kerala prawn curry

If you like spicy food, you'll love this curry, with its creamy consistency, crackling curry leaves and coconut flavour.

 20 minutes 2

- 2 red chillies, deseeded and quartered lengthways
- 1 small red onion, chopped
- 2.5cm/1in knob ginger, peeled and chopped
- 1 tbsp vegetable or sunflower oil
- 1 tsp black mustard seeds
- ½ tsp fenugreek seeds
- 14 curry leaves, fresh or dried
- ½ tsp turmeric powder
- ½ tsp cracked black peppercorns
- 150ml/¼ pint reduced-fat coconut milk
- 250g/9oz cooked and peeled jumbo prawns, some with their tails on
- squeeze lime
- chopped coriander leaves, plus a sprig or two, to garnish

1 In a food processor, blitz the chillies, onion and ginger with 3 tablespoons water to a smoothish paste.

2 Heat the oil in a wide shallow pan or wok. Toss in the mustard and fenugreek seeds and the curry leaves – they crackle and pop – and fry for 10 seconds. Add the onion paste, lower the heat and cook without colouring for about 5 minutes. Splash in some water, if it starts to catch.

3 Add the turmeric and peppercorns, and stir for a few seconds. Pour in the coconut milk and bring to a simmer, stirring all the time, then lower the heat and add the prawns. Cook for 1–2 minutes until heated through. Squeeze over some lime and sprinkle with coriander before serving, and garnish with a coriander sprig or two.

PER SERVING 294 kcals, protein 31g, carbs 8g, fat 16g, sat fat 8g, fibre none, sugar none, salt 2.76g

Creamy spiced mussels

Fresh mussels are surprisingly quick and easy to prepare. Serve this dish with bread to mop up the delicious juices.

 35 minutes   4

- 2kg/4lb 8oz fresh mussels
- 150ml/¼ pint dry white wine
- 2 shallots, finely chopped
- 25g/1oz butter
- 1 tsp plain flour
- 1–2 tsp curry paste
- 100ml/3½fl oz crème fraîche
- chopped parsley, to garnish

1 Scrub the mussels in a large bowl of cold water and discard any that are open. Put in a large pan with a lid with the wine. Bring to the boil, cover and shake the pan over a high heat until the mussels are open – about 3–4 minutes.

2 Tip the mussels into a colander set over a large bowl to catch the juices. Discard any that have not opened. Strain the cooking liquid through a sieve and reserve. Keep the mussels warm and set aside.

3 Fry the shallots in the butter in the large pan until softened. Stir in the flour and curry paste, and cook for 1 minute. Add the cooking liquid (except the last little bit, which may be gritty) and season with some black pepper, but no salt.

4 Stir in the crème fraîche and warm over a low heat until thick and glossy. Divide the mussels among four bowls and pour over the sauce. Scatter with parsley and serve.

PER SERVING 285 kcals, protein 19g, carbs 6g, fat 18g, sat fat 10g, fibre 1g, sugar none, salt 1.27g

Easiest-ever seafood risotto
· ·

Risottos make the perfect microwave one-pot dish. Unlike ones cooked on the hob, you don't have to stir, leaving you free to do something else.

 25–35 minutes   4

- 1 onion, finely chopped
- 1 fennel bulb, finely sliced
- 1 tbsp olive oil
- 300g/10oz risotto rice
- 500ml/18fl oz fish or vegetable stock
- 300g bag frozen seafood mix, defrosted
- 100g/4oz frozen peas
- 3 tbsp grated Parmesan
- grated zest and juice 1 lemon
- handful parsley leaves, roughly chopped

1 Tip the onion and fennel into a large microwave bowl, toss in the oil and microwave on High for 5 minutes. Stir in the rice, pour over the stock and cover the bowl with a plate. Microwave on High for 10–15 minutes more or until the rice is just on the verge of being cooked.

2 Stir in the seafood and peas, cover and continue to microwave on High for 2–3 minutes until the rice is cooked. Stir in the Parmesan and lemon juice, and leave to stand for a couple of minutes while you mix the parsley with the lemon zest. Spoon the risotto into bowls and scatter over the parsley and lemon zest. Serve.

· ·
PER SERVING 419 kcals, protein 29g, carbs 64g, fat 7g, sat fat 2g, fibre 4g, sugar none, salt 1.16g

Sizzling summer cod

You can use salmon instead of cod, if you like, in this fresh and tasty dish.

 15–20 minutes   2

- 250g jar roasted mixed peppers with herbs
- 250g/9oz new potatoes, scrubbed and thickly sliced
- 1 red onion, cut into wedges
- 140g/5oz green beans, trimmed and halved widthways
- 2 x 175g/6oz chunky cod fillets, skin on
- ½ lemon
- crusty bread, to serve

1 Pour all the oil from the jar of peppers into a deep frying pan with a lid. Heat the oil until bubbling, then tip in the potatoes and onion, and toss in the oil. Cook for 5 minutes, stirring every now and then, until the potatoes are beginning to turn golden.

2 Carefully pour most of the oil out of the frying pan, leaving behind about 1 tablespoon. Tip in the beans and drained peppers, season and stir until well mixed. Lay the fish, skin-side down, on top of the vegetables.

3 Cover the pan and cook over a medium heat for 5 minutes more or until the fish flakes easily with a fork and the vegetables are tender. Squeeze the lemon half over the fish and serve with crusty bread to mop up the juices.

PER SERVING 337 kcals, protein 37g, carbs 32g, fat 8g, sat fat 1g, fibre 5g, sugar none, salt 0.48g

Creamy haddock & tatties

· ·

This must be the easiest fish pie ever! There are only five ingredients and three simple steps, and the finished dish is very tasty indeed.

 15–20 minutes   2

- 400g/14oz smoked haddock (undyed is best, but not essential), skinned and chopped into chunks
- 1 trimmed leek, finely sliced
- handful parsley, chopped
- 142ml pot double cream
- 2 medium baking potatoes, about 200g/8oz each, unpeeled, sliced as thinly as possible

1 Scatter the haddock, leek and parsley over the base of a shallow microwave dish and mix together with your fingers or a spoon. Drizzle over half the cream and 5 tablespoon water. Lay the potato slices over the fish and leek. Season with a little salt and plenty of black pepper, and drizzle over the remaining cream.

2 Cover the dish with cling film and pierce a few times. Microwave on High for 8–10 minutes until everything is bubbling away and the potatoes are tender when pierced with a knife. While the dish is in the microwave, heat grill to high.

3 Remove the cling film and put the dish under the grill until the potatoes are golden. Leave to stand for a minute or two before serving.

· ·
PER SERVING 646 kcals, protein 45g, carbs 38g, fat 36g, sat fat 22g, fibre 4g, sugar none, salt 3.97g

Scallops with chilli & lime

Try this as a starter for a special meal for two.

 10–15 minutes 2

- 2 tbsp olive oil
- 10 scallops
- 2 large garlic cloves, chopped
- 2 tsp deseeded and chopped red chilli
- juice 1 lime
- small handful coriander leaves, roughly chopped, to garnish

1 Heat the oil in a non-stick frying pan until hot, add the scallops and pan-fry for 1 minute until golden underneath. Flip them over and sprinkle with the garlic and chilli.
2 Cook for 1 minute more, then pour over the lime juice and season with salt and black pepper. Serve immediately, scattered with the coriander.

PER SERVING 260 kcals, protein 34g, carbs 2g, fat 13g, sat fat 2g, fibre trace, sugar none, salt 0.99g

Smoked-haddock stovies

. . . .

Hearty and healthy, this is comfort food at its best – ideal for a midweek supper in the winter.

 30–35 minutes   4

- knob butter
- splash vegetable oil
- 2 onions, thinly sliced
- 1kg/2lb 4oz floury potatoes, such as Maris Piper or King Edward, peeled and thickly sliced
- 500g/1lb 2oz skinless smoked haddock, cut into large chunks
- handful parsley, coarsely chopped

1 Heat the butter and oil in a large wide pan, add the onions and cook for 5 minutes, stirring until lightly coloured. Tip in the potatoes and cook for a further 5 minutes, stirring often, until they are also lightly coloured.

2 Pour in 425ml/¾ pint water and grind in black pepper to taste. Stir to mix, then gently stir in the fish and bring to the boil. Cover and cook for 10 minutes or until the potatoes and fish are tender. Scatter with parsley before serving.

. . . .

PER SERVING 307 kcals, protein 29g, carbs 39g, fat 5g, sat fat 2g, fibre 4g, sugar none, salt 2.5g

Sausage & prawn jambalaya

Jambalaya means 'jumbled', and this creole dish is a lovely mix of meat and fish seasoned with the smoky flavour of paprika.

🕐 45 minutes   4

- 6 good-quality pork sausages (we used pork & chilli)
- sunflower oil, for frying
- 1 onion, chopped
- 1 red pepper, deseeded and chopped
- 2 garlic cloves, crushed
- 1 tbsp sweet smoked paprika
- 250g/9oz easy-cook long grain rice
- 400g can chopped tomatoes with garlic and herbs
- 400–500ml/14–18fl oz chicken stock
- 260g pack cooked and peeled king prawns

1 Fry the sausages in a large deep, lidded frying pan until golden all over, then remove and set aside. Heat a little of the oil (unless there is enough fat from the sausages already in the pan) and gently cook the onion for 5 minutes until soft.

2 Add the pepper, garlic and paprika, and cook for a few minutes more, then stir in the rice, mixing to coat all the grains well. Tip in the tomatoes and enough stock just to cover the rice. Simmer with the lid on for 10–12 minutes until the rice is tender. Add more stock if you need to during cooking.

3 About 5 minutes before the end of the cooking time, slice the sausages and return them to the pan. Cover and continue to cook until the rice is tender.

4 Stir through the prawns, put the lid on and leave to heat through. Season and serve immediately.

PER SERVING 626 kcals, protein 32g, carbs 74g, fat 21g, sat fat 7g, fibre 4g, sugar 9g, salt 2.9g

Spicy prawn & chorizo rice

An ever popular recipe for an easy and delicious one-pot meal.

 45–55 minutes 6

- 2 tbsp olive oil
- 2 garlic cloves, finely chopped
- 1 large onion, finely chopped
- 2 red chillies, deseeded and chopped
- 400g/14oz chorizo sausage, skinned and cut into chunks
- 450g/1lb long grain rice
- 1 tsp smoked paprika or 1 tbsp ground paprika
- 200ml/7fl oz dry white wine
- 1.5 litres/2¾ pints hot chicken stock (if using cubes, don't use more than two)
- 175g/6oz frozen broad beans or peas
- 400g/14oz raw peeled tiger prawns, thawed if frozen
- 250g/9oz cherry tomatoes, halved
- 3 tbsp chopped flat-leaf parsley, plus extra for sprinkling

1 Heat the oil in a wide shallow pan and fry the garlic, onion, chillies and chorizo for a few minutes until the onion has softened. Stir in the rice and paprika, then add the wine and bubble away until it evaporates.

2 Pour in the stock, lower the heat and cook gently for 10 minutes, stirring occasionally. Tip in the beans or peas, season and cook for 7–10 minutes, stirring, until the rice is tender. Keep some boiling water at the ready in case you need it to keep the rice moist.

3 Stir in the prawns and tomatoes, and cook for a few minutes until the prawns turn pink. Toss in the parsley and taste for seasoning before serving, sprinkled with a little more parsley.

PER SERVING 624 kcals, protein 33g, carbs 75g, fat 21g, sat fat 1g, fibre 3g, sugar none, salt 2.15g

Speedy salmon & leeks

Serve with crusty bread to mop up the tasty juices.

🕐 20–25 minutes   🍽 4

- 700g/1lb 9oz leeks, finely sliced
- 3 tbsp olive oil
- 2 tbsp wholegrain mustard
- 2 tbsp clear honey
- juice ½ lemon
- 250g pack cherry tomatoes, halved
- 4 x 175g/6oz skinless salmon fillets
- crusty bread, to serve

1 Put the leeks into a large microwave dish and sprinkle over 2 tablespoons water. Cover the dish with cling film and pierce a couple of times with a fork. Cook on High for 3 minutes, then leave to stand for 1 minute.

2 Whisk the olive oil, mustard, honey and lemon juice together to make a sauce, and season with a little salt and black pepper. Scatter the tomatoes on top of the leeks and spoon over half the sauce.

3 Lay the salmon fillets side by side on top of the vegetables and spoon the remaining sauce over them. Replace the cling film and continue cooking on High for 9 minutes. Leave to stand for a couple of minutes before serving with some crusty bread.

PER SERVING 471 kcals, protein 39g, carbs 13g, fat 29g, sat fat 6g, fibre 5g, sugar 6g, salt 0.54g

20-minute seafood pasta

For a Spanish-style version, add a pinch of saffron and a little white wine along with the tomatoes.

 20–25 minutes   4

- 1 tbsp olive oil
- 1 onion, chopped
- 1 garlic clove, chopped
- 1 tsp paprika
- 400g can chopped tomatoes
- 1 litre/1¾ pints chicken stock
- 300g/10oz spaghetti, roughly broken
- 240g pack mixed frozen seafood, defrosted
- handful parsley leaves, chopped, to garnish
- 4 lemon wedges, to squeeze over

1 Heat the oil in a wok or large frying pan, then cook the onion and garlic over a medium heat for 5 minutes until soft. Add the paprika, tomatoes and stock, then bring to the boil.
2 Turn down the heat to a simmer, stir in the pasta and cook for 7 minutes, stirring occasionally to stop the pasta from sticking.
3 Stir in the seafood, cook for 3 minutes more until it's all heated through and the pasta is cooked, then season to taste. Sprinkle with the parsley and serve with lemon wedges.

PER SERVING 370 kcals, protein 23g, carbs 62g, fat 5g, sat fat 1g, fibre 4g, sugar none, salt 1.4g

Vegetarian casserole

Make ahead to improve the flavour of this Mediterranean stew of peppers, courgettes, tomatoes and lentils. Then you can just reheat it when you want it.

🕐 50 minutes   4

- 1 tbsp olive or rapeseed oil
- 1 onion, finely chopped
- 3 garlic cloves, sliced
- 1 tsp smoked paprika
- ½ tsp ground cumin
- 1 tbsp dried thyme
- 3 medium carrots, sliced
- 2 medium celery sticks, finely sliced
- 1 red and 1 yellow pepper, deseeded and chopped
- 2 x 400g cans tomatoes or peeled cherry tomatoes
- 250ml/9fl oz vegetable stock
- 2 courgettes, sliced thickly
- 2 thyme sprigs
- 250g/9oz cooked lentils
- wild and white basmati rice, mash or quinoa, to serve

1. Heat the oil in a large heavy-based pan. Add the onion and cook gently for 5–10 minutes until softened. Add the garlic, spices, dried thyme, carrots, celery and peppers, and cook for 5 minutes. Add the tomatoes, vegetable stock, courgettes and thyme sprigs, and cook for 20–25 minutes.
2. Take out the thyme sprigs. Stir in the lentils and bring back to a simmer. Serve with wild and white basmati rice, mash or quinoa.

PER SERVING 216 kcals, protein 12g, carbs 31g, fat 51g, sat fat 1g, fibre 10g, sugar 16g, salt 1.6g

Potato & mozzarella tortilla

Use your own potato leftovers, if you like. Serve with a peppery rocket and watercress salad.

 30 minutes   6

- 2 tbsp olive oil
- 2 x 400g packs ready-roasted potatoes (available with different flavourings from most supermarkets)
- 8 eggs, beaten
- 4 vine-ripened tomatoes, sliced
- 150g ball mozzarella, torn into pieces

1 Heat the oil in a large ovenproof frying pan. Empty the potatoes into the pan, spread them out to cover the base, then fry for 5 minutes. Pour in the beaten eggs so they completely cover the potatoes, season well and leave the tortilla to cook on a medium heat for about 15–20 minutes, or until the base and edges have set.

2 Meanwhile, heat grill to high. Take the tortilla off the hob and put under the grill until the top is firm, then remove from the grill and scatter over the tomatoes and mozzarella. Put the tortilla back under the grill for a further 3–5 minutes, or until the tomatoes are soft and the cheese has melted. Serve hot or cold, cut into thick wedges.

PER SERVING 465 kcals, protein 28g, carbs 23g, fat 32g, sat fat 7g, fibre 3g, sugar none, salt 0.72g

Squash, lentil & bean spice-pot

Hit your 5-a-day with this easy-to-make curried-veggie spice-pot, which is packed with pulses and squash.

 45 minutes 2

- 400g/14oz piece butternut squash, peeled, deseeded and chunkily diced
- 1 onion, sliced
- 1 tbsp olive oil
- 2 tsp ground cumin
- ½ tsp chilli flakes
- 400g can chopped tomatoes
- 100g/4oz red split lentils
- 2 tsp agave syrup or brown sugar
- 2 tsp red or white wine vinegar
- 400g can kidney beans, drained and rinsed

FOR THE FIG RAITA
- 2 dried figs, finely chopped
- 150g pot fat-free natural yogurt
- ½ small bunch flat-leaf parsley, chopped

1 Fry the squash and onion in the oil for 5–8 minutes until the onion is softened. Stir in the cumin and chilli for 1 minute. Add the tomatoes plus a canful of water, the lentils, agave or sugar and the vinegar. Bring to a simmer and cook for 10 minutes, then stir in the beans and cook for a further few minutes until the lentils are tender and the beans heated through.

2 Meanwhile, mix the figs, yogurt and parsley together. Season the stew, then serve in bowls with the fig raita on the side.

PER SERVING 540 kcals, protein 28g, carbs 83g, fat 9g, sat fat 2g, fibre 15g, sugar 40g, salt 1.2g

Curried rice with spinach

Warming and tasty, practically no preparation, superhealthy, uses storecupboard ingredients – one-pot dishes don't get better than this.

 20 minutes   4

- 1 tbsp sunflower oil
- 2 garlic cloves, crushed
- 2 tbsp medium curry paste (Madras is a good one to use)
- 250g/9oz basmati rice, rinsed
- 450ml/16fl oz vegetable stock
- 400g can chickpeas, drained and rinsed
- handful raisins
- 175g/6oz frozen leaf spinach, thawed
- handful cashew nuts
- natural yogurt, to serve (optional)

1 Heat the oil in a large non-stick pan that has a lid, then fry the garlic and curry paste over a medium heat for 1 minute, until it smells toasty.

2 Tip the rice into the pan with the stock, chickpeas and raisins, and stir well with a fork to stop the rice from clumping. Season with salt and black pepper, then cover and bring to the boil. Reduce to a medium heat and cook for 12–15 minutes or until all the liquid has been absorbed and the rice is tender.

3 Squeeze the excess water from the thawed spinach with your hands. Tip it into the pan along with 2 tablespoons hot water, then fluff up the rice with a fork, making sure the spinach is mixed in well. Toss in the cashews. Serve drizzled with natural yogurt, if you like.

PER SERVING 380 kcals, protein 12g, carbs 66g, fat 9g, sat fat 1g, fibre 4g, sugar none, salt 1.02g

Vegetable casserole with dumplings

The wine really adds flavour to this warming dish, and the baby vegetables look so pretty, too.

 1¾–2 hours   6

- 8 shallots, halved lengthways
- 3 tbsp light olive oil
- 250g/9oz new potatoes, halved
- 1 chilli, deseeded and chopped
- 200g/8oz baby carrots, scraped
- 500g/1lb 2oz fennel, cut into wedges
- 300ml/½ pint fruity white wine
- 600ml/1 pint vegetable stock
- 200g/8oz green beans, halved
- 250g/9oz mushrooms, halved
- 200g/8oz baby courgettes, chopped
- 1 tbsp each snipped chives and chopped parsley

FOR THE DUMPLINGS

- 50g/2oz butter, cut into pieces
- 100g/4oz self-raising flour
- 50g/2oz mature Cheddar, grated
- 3 tbsp finely chopped parsley leaves

1 Fry the shallots in the oil in a flameproof casserole until softened. Add the potatoes and fry for 5–7 minutes, then add the chilli, carrots and fennel, and fry until coloured. Pour in the wine and stock, and bring to the boil. Season, cover and simmer for 10 minutes.
2 Make the dumplings. Rub the butter into the flour, stir in the cheese, parsley and some seasoning, then stir in about 2 tablespoons water to form a soft dough. Break off small pieces and form into 20–25 dumplings.
3 Add the beans to the pan and simmer for 5 minutes, then add the mushrooms and courgettes. Bring to the boil and stir well. Put the dumplings on top. Cover and simmer for 15 minutes until the dumplings have risen. Taste for seasoning and serve sprinkled with the chives and parsley.

PER SERVING 285 kcals, protein 8g, carbs 28g, fat 17g, sat fat 7g, fibre 6g, sugar none, salt 0.85g

Greek salad omelette

Juicy tomatoes and creamy cheese ensure a dish with flavours that will burst in your mouth.

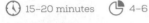 15–20 minutes   4–6

- 10 eggs
- handful parsley leaves, chopped
- 2 tbsp olive oil
- 1 large red onion, cut into wedges
- 3 tomatoes, chopped into large chunks
- large handful black olives (pitted are easier to eat)
- 100g/4oz feta, crumbled

1 Heat grill to high. Whisk the eggs in a large bowl with the chopped parsley, and some black pepper, and salt, if you want. Heat the oil in a large, non-stick ovenproof frying pan, then fry the onion wedges over a high heat for about 4 minutes until they start to brown around the edges. Add the tomatoes and olives, stir and cook for 1–2 minutes until the tomatoes begin to soften.

2 Turn the heat down to medium and pour in the eggs. Stir the eggs as they begin to set, until half cooked but still runny in places – about 2 minutes. Scatter over the feta, then slide the pan under the grill for 5–6 minutes until the omelette is puffed up and golden. Cut into wedges and serve straight from the pan.

PER SERVING (4) 371 kcals, protein 24g, carbs 5g, fat 28g, sat fat 9g, fibre 1g, sugar none, salt 2g

Easy ratatouille with poached eggs

This gutsy dish can be prepared in advance. Cook until the end of step 2, then gently reheat later and crack in the eggs.

 1 hour 5 minutes   4

- 1 tbsp olive oil
- 1 large onion, chopped
- 1 red or orange pepper, deseeded and thinly sliced
- 2 garlic cloves, finely chopped
- 1 tbsp chopped rosemary leaves
- 1 aubergine, diced
- 2 courgettes, diced
- 400g can chopped tomatoes
- 1 tsp balsamic vinegar
- 4 eggs
- handful basil leaves
- crusty bread, to serve

1 Heat the oil in a large frying pan with a lid. Add the onion, pepper, garlic and rosemary, then cook for 5 minutes, stirring frequently, until the onion has softened. Add the aubergine and courgettes, then cook for 2 minutes more.

2 Add the tomatoes, then fill the can with water, swirl it around and tip into the pan. Bring to the boil, cover, then simmer for 40 minutes, uncovering after 20 minutes, or until the sauce is reduced and pulpy.

3 Stir the vinegar into the ratatouille, then make four spaces for the eggs. Crack an egg into each hole and season with black pepper. Cover, then cook for 2–5 minutes until set as softly or firmly as you like. Scatter over the basil and serve with some crusty bread to mop up the juices.

PER SERVING 190 kcals, protein 12g, carbs 13g, fat 11g, sat fat 2g, fibre 5g, sugar 10g, salt 0.36g

Spring-vegetable pilaf

Use whichever vegetables are in season for this light and pretty dish. To make it richer, add 100g/4oz feta when you stir in the dill.

 20 minutes   4

- 1 tbsp olive oil
- 1 onion, chopped
- 300g/10oz basmati rice
- 700ml/1¼ pints vegetable stock
- 100g pack asparagus, cut into 2cm/¾in chunks
- large handful peas, fresh or frozen
- large handful broad beans, fresh or frozen
- 1 courgette, sliced
- small bunch dill, chopped

1 Heat the oil in a frying pan with a lid and cook the onion for 5 minutes until soft. Tip in the rice, pour over the stock and stir. Bring to the boil, then lower the heat to a simmer, cover and cook for 10 minutes or until the rice is almost tender.

2 Add the vegetables to the pan, cover and let them steam for 2 minutes. Take the pan off the heat and leave to stand, covered, for another 2 minutes to absorb any more liquid. Stir in the dill just before serving.

PER SERVING 317 kcals, protein 9g, carbs 66g, fat 4g, sat fat 1g, fibre 3g, sugar none, salt 0.58g

Chipotle-bean chilli with baked eggs
. . . .

Chipotle chilli paste adds an authentic smoky Mexican flavour. If you can't find it in the supermarket, it's easily bought online.

 35 minutes 4

- 1 tbsp sunflower oil
- 1 onion, chopped
- 1–2 tbsp chipotle paste (depending on how hot you like it)
- 2 x 400g cans black beans, drained and rinsed
- 400g can mixed beans, drained and rinsed
- 2 x 400g cans chopped tomatoes with garlic and herbs
- 1 heaped tbsp brown sugar
- 4 eggs
- small handful coriander leaves
- soured cream and warm flour tortillas, to serve

1 Heat the oil in a deep frying pan and cook the onion for about 5 minutes until soft. Add the chipotle paste, beans, tomatoes and sugar, and simmer for about 15–20 minutes until thickened. Season to taste.
2 Make four holes in the tomato-and-bean mixture and crack an egg into each one. Cover and simmer over a low heat for 8–10 minutes until the eggs are cooked to your liking.
3 Sprinkle over the coriander leaves and serve with a bowl of soured cream and some warm flour tortillas.

. . . .
PER SERVING 377 kcals, protein 24g, carbs 48g, fat 10g, sat fat 2g, fibre 15g, sugar 21g, salt 0.5g

Mixed-vegetable balti

Serve with warm mini naan breads. Alternatively this curry mixture makes a great low-fat filling for baked potatoes.

 1¼–1½ hours 4

- 1 tbsp vegetable oil
- 1 large onion, thickly sliced
- 1 large garlic clove, crushed
- 1 eating apple, peeled, cored and chopped into chunks
- 3 tbsp balti curry paste
- 1 medium butternut squash, peeled and cut into chunks
- 2 large carrots, thickly sliced
- 200g/8oz turnips, cut into chunks
- 1 cauliflower, about 500g/1lb 2oz, broken into florets
- 400g can chopped tomatoes
- 425ml/¾ pint vegetable stock
- 4 tbsp chopped coriander leaves, plus extra to garnish
- 150g carton low-fat natural yogurt
- mini naan breads, to serve

1 Heat the oil in a large pan with a lid and cook the onion, garlic and apple gently, stirring occasionally, until the onion softens – about 5–8 minutes. Stir in the curry paste.
2 Tip the fresh vegetables, tomatoes and stock into the pan. Stir in 3 tablespoons of the coriander. Bring to the boil, lower the heat, cover and cook for 30 minutes.
3 Remove the lid and cook for another 20 minutes until the vegetables are soft and the liquid has reduced a little. Season with salt and pepper.
4 Mix the remaining coriander into the yogurt to make a raita. Ladle the curry into bowls, drizzle over some raita and sprinkle with extra coriander. Serve with the remaining raita and some warm mini naan breads.

PER SERVING 201 kcals, protein 11g, carbs 25g, fat 7g, sat fat 1g, fibre 7g, sugar none, salt 1.13g

Oven egg & chips

Want to be practical but need some inspiration? This dish is a great way of using up potatoes and it's not as unhealthy as it looks.

 1 hour   2

- 450g/1lb floury potatoes, such as King Edward or Maris Piper
- 2 garlic cloves, sliced
- 4 rosemary sprigs or 1 tsp dried rosemary
- 2 tbsp olive oil
- 2 eggs

1 Heat oven to 220C/200C fan/gas 7. Without peeling, cut the potatoes into thick chips. Tip them into a roasting tin (non-stick is best) and scatter over the garlic. Strip the rosemary leaves from the sprigs and sprinkle them, or the dried rosemary, over too. Drizzle with the oil, season well, then toss the chips to coat them in oil and flavourings.

2 Oven-roast the chips for 35–40 minutes until just cooked and golden, shaking the tin halfway through.

3 Make two gaps in the chips and break an egg into each gap. Return to the oven for 3–5 minutes until the eggs are cooked to your liking.

PER SERVING 348 kcals, protein 11g, carbs 40g, fat 17g, sat fat 3g, fibre 3g, sugar none, salt 0.22g

Spiced carrot, chickpea & almond pilaf

A rice dish with North African flavours that works equally well as a vegetarian main course or side dish.

 40 minutes  4

- 1 tbsp olive oil
- 2 onions, finely chopped
- 3 carrots (about 300g/10oz total), coarsely grated
- 2 tbsp harissa paste
- 300g/10oz basmati rice, rinsed
- 700ml/1¼ pints vegetable stock, made with 1 stock cube (or equivalent)
- 400g can chickpeas, drained and rinsed
- 25g/1oz toasted flaked almonds
- 200g pot Greek yogurt

1 Heat the oil in a lidded casserole dish. Add the onions and cook for 8 minutes, until soft. Tip in the carrots, harissa and rice, and stir for a couple of minutes. Pour over the stock, bring to the boil, then cover with the lid and simmer for 10 minutes.

2 Fork through the chickpeas and cook gently for 3–5 minutes more, until the grains of rice are tender and all the liquid has been absorbed. Season, turn off the heat, cover and leave to sit for a few minutes.

3 Sprinkle the almonds over the rice mixture and serve with a dollop of yogurt.

PER SERVING 543 kcals, protein 15g, carbs 83g, fat 13g, sat fat 4g, fibre 7g, sugar 14g, salt 1.2g

Summer veggie & tofu bowl

Steaming is a great way of cooking food with flavourings. The results are light and tasty, and retain all the freshness of the ingredients.

 25 minutes   2

- 1–2 carrots, cut into sticks, if large
- 1–2 turnips, cut into wedges
- 1 tbsp dry sherry
- 2 tbsp soy sauce
- 1 courgette, cut into 1cm/½in slices
- 4–6 short asparagus spears
- 3 fresh shiitake or open-cup mushrooms, each sliced in 4
- 25g/1oz butter
- 2 spring onions, shredded
- 100g/4oz smoked tofu, cubed

1 Mix the carrot and turnip with the sherry and soy sauce in a shallow heatproof bowl that will fit inside a steamer basket. Leave to marinate for 10 minutes.
2 Bring a pan of water to the boil, fit the steamer basket, then put the bowl of carrot and turnip inside. Cover and steam for 4–5 minutes.
3 Add the courgette, asparagus and mushrooms, stirring to mix. Dot with the butter sprinkle with the spring onions, cover and continue steaming for another 3 minutes.
4 Add the tofu and continue steaming for 2 minutes. Remove the bowl and mix everything together before serving.

PER SERVING 206 kcals, protein 8g, carbs 11g, fat 13g, sat fat 7g, fibre 4g, sugar trace, salt 3.01g

Cheesy vegetable hotpot

This is vegetarian food at its easiest and most comforting.

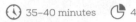 35–40 minutes 4

- 3 leeks, trimmed, roughly sliced
- large knob butter
- ½ small Savoy cabbage, shredded
- 8 chestnut mushrooms, sliced
- 4 tbsp crème fraîche
- 3 medium potatoes, peeled and thinly sliced
- 1 small Camembert or other rinded soft cheese, sliced with the rind on
- 1 tbsp thyme leaves

1 In a shallow microwavable dish, toss the leeks in half the butter and microwave on High for 5 minutes until they begin to soften. Stir in the cabbage and mushrooms, and add the crème fraîche. Lay the potato slices over the vegetables, pressing them down with a fish slice.
2 Dot the potatoes with the remaining butter and microwave, uncovered, for 15–20 minute on High until they are done. Scatter over the cheese and thyme, and either microwave on High to melt for 2 minutes, or put under a high grill until crisp and brown. Leave to stand for a few minutes before serving.

PER SERVING 308 kcals, protein 15g, carbs 19g, fat 20g, sat fat 12g, fibre 5g, sugar none, salt 0.83g

Chilli Marrakesh

. . . .

If you love spicy, aromatic dishes, this supper for a crowd will instantly become a favourite. If you're not cooking for many, stick to the recipe and freeze half.

🕐 1½ hours, plus heating from frozen 🥧 10

- 1½ tbsp cumin seeds
- 1 tbsp olive oil
- 3 onions, halved and thinly sliced
- 3 x 400g packs lean lamb mince
- 2 tbsp finely chopped ginger
- 4 garlic cloves, finely chopped
- 2 x 400g cans chopped tomatoes
- 1 tbsp each paprika and ground cinnamon
- 1½ tbsp ground coriander
- 3 tbsp harissa paste, plus extra if you like it spicy
- 3 red peppers, deseeded and cut into large chunks
- 2 x 400g cans chickpeas, drained and rinsed
- 2 x 20g packs coriander, most chopped, a few leaves left whole to garnish
- 500ml/18fl oz beef or lamb stock, made with 2 cubes

1 Heat your largest non-stick wok or pan over a high heat, tip in the cumin seeds and toast for a few seconds. Remove to a plate. Add the oil to the pan and fry the onions for 5 minutes until starting to colour. Add the mince, ginger and garlic, and cook, breaking up the mince with your wooden spoon, until the meat is no longer pink. Drain any excess liquid or fat from the pan.

2 Stir in the tomatoes, toasted cumin seeds, remaining spices and harissa – add more if you like an extra kick. Add the peppers, chickpeas, three-quarters of the chopped coriander and the stock. Cover and cook for 40 minutes, stirring occasionally, until the sauce is slightly thickened. Remove from the heat. Cool a little, then stir in the remaining chopped coriander. Serve, or pack into freezer bags and store for up to 3 months. To serve, transfer to a pan and heat from frozen on the hob with a little water until bubbling hot, then scatter with coriander.

. . . .

PER SERVING 357 kcals, protein 28g, carbs 17g, fat 19g, sat fat 8g, fibre 5g, sugar 7g, salt 1.2g

Chicken with spring vegetables

Play around with this recipe. If you don't feel like using asparagus and broad beans, you could try broccoli sprigs and green beans instead.

 1¼–1½ hours   8

- 2 tbsp olive oil
- 25g/1oz butter
- 8 large boneless skinless chicken breasts
- 8 shallots, halved
- 2 garlic cloves, roughly chopped
- 450g/1lb baby new potatoes, halved
- 450g/1lb baby carrots, scrubbed
- 3 tbsp plain flour
- 1½ tbsp Dijon mustard
- 425ml/¾ pint dry white wine
- 425ml/¾ pint chicken stock
- 200g/8oz asparagus tips, trimmed
- 200g/8oz shelled broad beans, thawed if frozen
- 1 tbsp lemon juice
- 100ml/3½ fl oz double cream
- handful chopped mixed fresh parsley and tarragon leaves
- crusty bread, to serve

1 Heat the oil and butter in a large pan with a lid. Cut each chicken breast into three pieces, add to the pan then cook in batches for 3–4 minutes until golden all over. Remove from the pan to a plate. Add the shallots, garlic, potatoes and carrots to the pan, and toss together. Cook for about 5 minutes until beginning to turn golden. Sprinkle over the flour, stir in the mustard and toss well, then pour over the white wine and gently simmer until reduced by about half.

2 Pour in the stock, bring to a simmer, then return the chicken to the pan. Cover and simmer for about 15 minutes.

3 Scatter over the asparagus and broad beans without stirring, cover and simmer for a further 8 minutes. Stir in the lemon juice, cream, parsley and tarragon, and heat through gently. Serve with crusty bread.

PER SERVING 414 kcals, protein 42g, carbs 23g, fat 14g, sat fat 6g, fibre 5g, sugar none, salt 0.92g

Chinese-style braised beef

We used ox cheek in this recipe – if you can get it, it is fantastic value and rich in flavour, making it perfect for braising in a dish like this.

 2 hours 20 minutes  6

- 3–4 tbsp olive oil
- 6 garlic cloves, thinly sliced
- good thumb-sized knob ginger, peeled and shredded
- 1 bunch spring onions, sliced
- 1 red chilli, deseeded and thinly sliced
- 1.5kg/3lb 5oz braising beef, cut into large pieces
- 2 tbsp plain flour, well seasoned
- 1 tsp Chinese five-spice powder
- 2 star anise (optional)
- 2 tsp light muscovado sugar (or use whatever you've got)
- 3 tbsp Chinese cooking wine or dry sherry
- 3 tbsp dark soy sauce, plus more to season
- 500ml/18fl oz beef stock
- steamed pak choi and steamed basmati rice, to serve

1 Heat 2 tablespoons of the oil in a large shallow casserole dish. Fry the garlic, ginger, onions and chilli for 3 minutes until soft. Tip on to a plate. Toss the beef in the flour, add 1 tablespoon more oil to the pan, then brown the meat in batches, for about 5 minutes each. Add the final tablespoon oil if needed.

2 Add the five-spice and star anise (if using) to the pan, tip in the gingery mix, then fry for 1 minute until the spices are fragrant. Add the sugar, then the beef and stir until combined. Keep the heat high, then splash in the wine or sherry, scraping up any meaty bits. Heat oven to 150C/130C fan/gas 2.

3 Pour in the soy and stock, bring to a simmer, then tightly cover, transfer to the oven and cook for 1–2 hours, stirring the meat halfway through. The meat should be very soft, and any sinewy bits should have melted away. Season with more soy. This can now be chilled and frozen for up to 1 month.

4 Nestle the cooked pak choi into the pan then serve straight away with the basmati rice.

PER SERVING 513 kcals, protein 54g, carbs 9g, fat 29g, sat fat 10g, fibre 1g, sugar 4g, salt 2.39g

Hob-to-table moussaka

· ·

This is a quick variation of the classic Greek dish. For an authentic Mediterranean meal, serve with toasted pitta bread.

 40–50 minutes   8

- 2 tbsp olive oil
- 2 large onions, finely chopped
- 2 garlic cloves, finely chopped
- 1kg/2lb 4oz minced lamb
- 2 x 400g cans chopped tomatoes
- 3 tbsp tomato purée
- 2 tsp ground cinnamon
- 200g jar chargrilled aubergines in olive oil, drained and chopped
- 300g/10oz feta, crumbled
- large handful mint leaves, chopped
- green salad and toasted pitta bread, to serve

1 Heat the oil in a large deep frying pan. Toss in the onions and garlic, and fry until soft. Add the mince and stir-fry for about 10 minutes until browned.

2 Tip the tomatoes into the pan, add a canful of water and stir in the tomato purée and cinnamon. Season generously with salt and pepper. Leave the mince to simmer for 30 minutes, adding the aubergines halfway through.

3 Sprinkle the crumbled feta and chopped mint over the mince. Bring the moussaka to the table as the feta melts, and serve with a crunchy green salad and toasted pitta.

· ·

PER SERVING 454 kcals, protein 32g, carbs 10g, fat 32g, sat fat 14g, fibre 2g, sugar none, salt 1.83g

Thai green chicken curry

Thai curries cook in just a few minutes once all the ingredients are prepared, so this is a one-pot dish you'll be cooking again and again.

 30–40 minutes   8

- 2 tbsp vegetable oil
- 2 garlic cloves, chopped
- 6 tsp Thai green curry paste
- 2 x 400ml cans coconut milk
- 450g/1lb new potatoes, scrubbed and cut into chunks
- 200g pack trimmed green beans, halved
- 4 tsp Thai fish sauce, or to taste
- 2 tsp caster sugar
- 6 boneless skinless chicken breasts, cut into large bite-sized pieces
- 2 fresh kaffir lime leaves, finely shredded, or 3 wide strips lime zest
- large handful basil leaves

1 Heat the oil in a large wok, drop in the garlic and stir until just golden. Add the curry paste and stir for a couple of minutes, then pour in the coconut milk and bring to the boil. Add the potatoes and simmer for 10 minutes, then add the beans and simmer for 5 minutes more. Both the potatoes and beans should be just tender by now – if not, cook a little longer.
2 Stir in the fish sauce and sugar, then add the chicken, cover and simmer for 10 minutes until tender. Before serving, stir in the lime leaves or zest, followed by the basil. Taste and add more fish sauce if you like.

PER SERVING 363 kcals, protein 29g, carbs 15g, fat 21g, sat fat 15g, fibre 1g, sugar 1g, salt 1.09g

Pot-roast veal with new-season carrots & orange

· ·

To guarantee the veal has been humanely reared, only buy a British rose veal, which is raised outdoors.

 3 hours   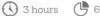 6

- 1.5kg/3lb 5oz piece rolled and tied British rose veal shoulder
- 3 garlic cloves, 1 finely sliced, 2 bashed
- bunch thyme
- 1 tbsp olive oil
- 25g/1oz butter
- 800g/1lb 12oz new-season bunch carrots, trimmed with stalks still attached
- 1 large shallot, roughly chopped
- sprinkling icing sugar
- zest 1 orange, ½ pared into strips, ½ finely grated
- 150ml/¼ pint white wine
- 350ml/12fl oz chicken stock

1 Heat oven to 180C/160C fan/gas 4. Stud the gaps in the veal joint with the sliced garlic and some of the thyme, then season well.

2 Heat the oil and butter in a deep flameproof casserole dish then slowly sizzle the veal for 15 minutes, until brown all over. Remove the joint to a plate and add the carrots, shallot and icing sugar, then cook for 5 minutes until everything is slightly caramelised. Lift out the carrots but leave everything else in the dish. Add the rest of the thyme, the bashed garlic and pared orange zest. Nestle the veal back in the dish and pour over the wine, then the stock. Cover and put in the oven for 1 hour.

3 Remove the dish from the oven, uncover, and scatter the carrots around the meat. Return the dish to the oven for 1 hour, uncovered. Cook until the meat is very tender, then leave to cool slightly. Lift the meat on to a board and carve into slices. Serve with the juices from the dish and the tender carrots.

· ·

PER SERVING 425 kcals, protein 44g, carbs 10g, fat 20g, sat fat 8g, fibre 5g, sugar 9g, salt 0.8g

Slow-braised pork shoulder with cider & parsnips

Shoulder of pork is the ideal cut for this warming one-pot, as the ratio of meat to fat means not only that it won't dry out but also that it won't make the juices too fatty.

 2 hours 50 minutes   6

- 2 tbsp olive oil
- 1kg/2lb 4oz pork shoulder, diced
- 2 onions, sliced
- 2 celery sticks, roughly chopped
- 3 parsnips, cut into chunks
- 2 bay leaves
- 1 tbsp plain flour
- 330ml bottle cider
- 850ml/1½ pints chicken stock
- handful parsley leaves, chopped
- mashed potato and greens, to serve (optional)

1 Heat oven to 180C/160C fan/gas 4. Heat the oil in a large lidded, flameproof casserole dish and brown the meat in batches, then remove to a plate. Add the onions, celery and parsnips with the bay leaves to the casserole dish and fry for 10 minutes until golden brown. Sprinkle in the flour and give a good stir, then add the pork and any juices back to the dish.

2 Add the cider and stock so that the meat and vegetables are covered. Season and bring to a simmer, then cover and cook in the oven for 2 hours.

3 Serve sprinkled with parsley alongside some mashed potato and greens, if you like.

PER SERVING 534 kcals, protein 46g, carbs 19g, fat 29g, sat fat 9g, fibre 8g, sugar 10g, salt 0.8g

Chicken with goat's cheese

This dish tastes rather special for something that's so easy to make. As an alternative to goat's cheese you can use Boursin.

 40–50 minutes   8

- 8 large skinless chicken breasts
- 20g pack tarragon
- 2 x 150g cartons soft goat's cheese, such as Charvoux
- 5 vine-ripened tomatoes, sliced
- 3 tbsp olive oil
- dressed salad leaves and bread, to serve

1 Heat oven to 200C/180C fan/gas 6. Make a slit down the centre of each chicken breast (taking care not to cut right through), then make a pocket with your fingers. Arrange the chicken in a single layer in a large, lightly oiled ovenproof dish.

2 Reserve 8 sprigs of the tarragon, chop the rest of the leaves and beat into the cheese with plenty of black pepper. Spoon into the pockets in the chicken. Put 2 of the tomato slices over each cheese-filled pocket, pop a tarragon sprig on top and drizzle with oil.

3 Season and bake for 25–30 minutes until the chicken is cooked, but still moist. Serve hot or cold with dressed salad leaves and bread.

PER SERVING 248 kcals, protein 34g, carbs 2g, fat 12g, sat fat 4g, fibre 1g, sugar none, salt 0.64g

Beef & bean hotpot

This is a brilliant way of stretching a couple of packets of mince.

🕐 1 hour 🥧 8

- 750g/1lb 10oz lean minced beef
- 1 beef stock cube
- 2 large onions, roughly chopped
- 450g/1lb carrots, peeled and thickly sliced
- 1.25kg/2lb 8oz potatoes, peeled and cut into large chunks
- 2 x 400g cans baked beans
- Worcestershire or Tabasco sauce, to taste
- large handful parsley leaves, roughly chopped, to garnish

1 Heat a large non-stick pan, add the beef and fry over a medium–high heat until browned, stirring often and breaking up any lumps with a spoon. Crumble in the stock cube and mix well.

2 Add the vegetables, stir to mix with the beef and pour in enough boiling water (about 1.2 litres/2 pints) to cover. Bring to the boil, then lower the heat and stir well. Cover the pan and simmer gently for about 30 minutes or until the vegetables are tender.

3 Tip in the baked beans, sprinkle with Worcestershire or Tabasco sauce to taste, stir well and heat through. Taste for seasoning and sprinkle with the parsley. Serve with extra Worcestershire or Tabasco sauce, for those who like a peppery hot taste.

PER SERVING 362 kcals, protein 31g, carbs 51g, fat 5g, sat fat 2g, fibre 8g, sugar 3g, salt 2.05g

Guinea-fowl tagine with chickpeas, squash & apricots

It's easy to go down the traditional route with birds like guinea fowl. However, they are just as suited to global dishes like curries – or this tagine.

 1 hour 40 minutes   6

- 3 tbsp olive oil
- 2 guinea fowl, jointed like a chicken (you can ask your butcher to do this)
- 2 onions, roughly chopped
- 1 butternut squash
- 2 garlic cloves, chopped
- 1 tbsp ras-el-hanout
- 1 tsp ground cumin
- 1 tsp ground coriander
- ½ tsp ground ginger
- 1 large cinnamon stick
- small squeeze clear honey
- large pinch saffron, soaked in 1 tbsp boiling water
- juice 1 lemon
- 850ml/1½ pints chicken stock
- 400g can chickpeas, drained and rinsed
- 200g/7oz dried apricots
- bunch coriander, chopped

1 Heat the oil in a large shallow, flameproof casserole dish. Season the guinea-fowl pieces and brown them – in batches, if necessary – then remove to a plate.

2 Fry the onions in the same dish until softened. Peel, deseed and cut the butternut squash into large chunks then add with the garlic to the dish, cooking for 1–2 minutes. Tip in the spices and cook for a few minutes before adding the honey, saffron and its soaking water and the lemon juice. Pour in the chicken stock and the chickpeas.

3 Submerge the guinea-fowl pieces in the stock and add the apricots. Cover the dish and simmer everything very gently for 50 minutes–1 hour, until the fowl and squash are both tender. Stir through the coriander and serve.

PER SERVING 591 kcals, protein 64g, carbs 31g, fat 22g, sat fat 5g, fibre 6g, sugar 20g, salt 1.1g

Mexican beef chilli

The amount of chilli paste used in this recipe is suitable for a medium heat; add more or less according to your taste.

 2½ hours 15 Easily halved

- up to 6 tbsp sunflower oil
- 4kg/9lb stewing beef, cut into chunks
- 4 onions, sliced
- 4 tbsp chipotle paste
- 8 garlic cloves, crushed
- 50g/2oz knob ginger, grated
- 1 tbsp ground cumin
- 2 tsp ground cinnamon
- 1 tbsp plain flour
- 2 litres/3½ pints beef stock
- 3 x 400g cans chopped tomatoes
- 1 tbsp dried oregano
- 5 x 400g cans pinto or kidney beans, drained

1 Heat a small drizzle of the oil in an extra-large flameproof dish. Brown the meat in batches, adding a drop more oil when needed, then remove from the dish to a plate. Add 1 tablespoon of the oil to the dish, then the onions, and cook for 7–10 minutes or until caramelised.

2 Stir the chipotle paste, garlic, ginger, cumin, cinnamon and flour in with the onions, and cook for a couple of minutes. Gradually add the stock, stirring all the time, so it's fully mixed in with the other ingredients. Add the tomatoes and oregano, then season and simmer for 10 minutes.

3 Now tip in the beef, cover and simmer very gently for about 1¾ hours until tender, removing the lid and adding the beans for the final 15 minutes. If the sauce is thin, let it boil down for a further 5–10 minutes with the lid off. Before serving, adjust the seasoning.

PER SERVING 551 kcals, protein 69g, carbs 19g, fat 22g, sat fat 8g, fibre 7g, sugar 6g, salt 1.7g

Beef paprikash

A comforting and hearty dish that's perfect for winter dinner parties.

 3–3½ hours   8

- 3 tbsp sunflower oil
- 1.5kg/3lb braising steak or stewing beef, cut into 5cm/2in cubes
- 2 large onions, sliced
- 2 garlic cloves, crushed
- 2 rounded tbsp paprika
- 3 tbsp tomato purée
- 2 tbsp wine vinegar (red or white)
- 2 tsp dried marjoram or mixed herbs
- 2 bay leaves
- ½ tsp caraway seeds
- 2 x 400g cans chopped tomatoes or 2 x 500g jars passata
- 750ml/1¼ pints beef stock
- 2 large red peppers, deseeded and cut into rings
- 142ml carton soured cream, to serve

1 Heat oven to 160C/140C fan/gas 3. Heat 2 tablespoons of the oil in a large flameproof casserole until very hot. Brown the meat in 2–3 batches, removing each batch to a plate with a slotted spoon.

2 Add the remaining oil, the onions and garlic. Cook on a low heat for 10 minutes, stirring now and then, until the onions soften. Add the meat and juices, and blend in the paprika, tomato purée, vinegar, herbs, bay leaves and caraway seeds.

3 Tip in the tomatoes or passata, add the stock, season and bring to the boil, adding some water if the meat is not covered. Stir, cover and put in the oven for 2½ hours, or until the meat is tender. Halfway through, stir in the red peppers. Serve with dollops of soured cream.

PER SERVING 451 kcals, protein 43g, carbs 14g, fat 25g, sat fat 10g, fibre 3g, sugar none, salt 0.87g

Fragrant chicken curry

Impress your friends with this sensational curry, which delivers a full rich flavour and authentic spiciness without the usual high-fat content.

 1 hour 8

- 3 onions, quartered
- 4 fat garlic cloves
- 5cm/2in knob ginger, peeled and roughly chopped
- 3 tbsp moglai (medium) curry powder
- 1 tsp turmeric powder
- 2 tsp paprika
- 2 red chillies, deseeded and roughly chopped
- 2 x 20g packs coriander
- 1 chicken stock cube
- 6 large boneless skinless chicken breasts, cubed
- 2 x 410g cans chickpeas, drained and rinsed
- low-fat natural yogurt, naan bread or poppadums, to serve

1 Tip the onions, garlic, ginger, curry powder, ground spices, chillies and half the coriander into a food processor. Add 1 teaspoon salt and blend to a purée (you may need to do this in two batches). Tip the mixture into a large pan and cook over a low heat for 10 minutes, stirring frequently.

2 Crumble in the stock cube, pour in 750ml/ 1¼ pints boiling water and return to the boil. Add the chicken, stir, then lower the heat and simmer for 20 minutes or until the chicken is tender.

3 Chop the remaining coriander, then stir all but about 2 tablespoons into the curry with the chickpeas. Heat through. Serve topped with the reserved coriander and the natural yogurt, with naan bread or poppadums on the side.

PER SERVING 227 kcals, protein 32g, carbs 17g, fat 4g, sat fat trace, fibre 5g, sugar none, salt 1.72g

Lamb & red pepper stew

Tender neck fillets of lamb are more expensive than pre-diced casserole lamb but do cut down on cooking time.

 1 hour 8

- 1.25kg/2lb 8oz boneless lamb fillet, cut into small chunks
- 40g/1½oz plain flour, seasoned
- 3 tbsp olive oil
- 3 garlic cloves, crushed
- 300ml/½ pint dry white wine
- 3 large red peppers, deseeded and cut into 5cm/2in pieces
- 500g jar passata
- 300ml/½ pint stock (lamb, chicken or vegetable)
- 3 bay leaves
- 175g/6oz ready-to-eat dried prunes or apricots

1 Coat the lamb in the seasoned flour, shaking off the excess. Heat 2 tablespoons of the oil in a large pan until hot. Tip in a third of the lamb and fry over a medium–high heat, turning occasionally, until browned. Transfer to a plate with a slotted spoon and repeat with the remaining lamb, adding the remaining o when necessary.

2 Return all the meat to the pan, sprinkle in the garlic and cook for 1 minute. Pour in the wine and, scraping up any residue, cook over a high heat until reduced by about a third. Stir in all the remaining ingredients except the dried fruit. Cover and simmer for 30–40 minutes or until the lamb is tender.

3 Stir in the dried fruit and heat through for 5 minutes, then taste for seasoning before serving.

PER SERVING 497 kcals, protein 31g, carbs 22g, fat 32g, sat fat 15g, fibre 3g, sugar 1g, salt 0.69g

Beaujolais berries

Marinating the strawberries in the Beaujolais gives them a lovely flavour, but don't do it too far ahead or they will lose their texture.

 5 minutes, plus marinating  6

- 700g/1lb 9oz strawberries, hulled and halved
- 3 tbsp golden caster sugar
- handful mint leaves, plus a few extra to scatter
- 75cl bottle Beaujolais

1 Lay the strawberries in a bowl and sprinkle over the caster sugar. Scatter over a handful of mint leaves and let the strawberries sit for about 30 minutes so they start to release their juices.
2 Pour the Beaujolais over the strawberries and scatter over a few more mint leaves. Leave for another 10 minutes before serving.

PER SERVING 102 kcals, protein 1g, carbs 15g, fat 1g, sat fat none, fibre 1g, sugar 8g, salt 0.03g

Cookie-dough crumble

To make this tasty pudding extra fruity, slice up a couple of pears or a cooking apple (with a sprinkling of sugar) and stir into the fruit.

 20–25 minutes 4

- 500g bag mixed frozen fruit
- 350g pot fresh cookie dough (chocolate chip is good)
- cream, ice cream or custard, to serve

1 Heat oven to 220C/200C fan/gas 7. Tip the frozen fruit into a shallow baking dish and tear pieces of dough all over the top.
2 Bake for 20 minutes until crisp and golden. Serve with cream, ice cream or custard.

PER SERVING 457 kcals, protein 8g, carbs 57g, fat 24g, sat fat 13g, fibre 6g, sugar 9g, salt 1.2g

Simple summer pudding

To make small puddings, simply tear the bread roughly and layer up with the fruit in individual ramekins. Turn out or serve as they are.

 40–50 minutes 4

- 450g/1lb summer berries, defrosted if frozen
- 4 tbsp blackcurrant cordial or crème de cassis
- 225g carton chilled red fruits compote
- 6 medium slices white bread, crusts cut off

1 Mix the berries, cordial or crème de cassis and compote, and leave for 5–10 minutes. If you are using defrosted fruit, mix in some of the juice.
2 Line a 1.2 litre pudding bowl with cling film, letting it hang over the sides. Cut a circle from one of the slices of bread to fit the base of the bowl, then cut the remaining slices into quarters.
3 Drain the juice from the fruit into a bowl and dip the bread into it until soaked. Layer the fruit and bread in the bowl, and pour over the remaining juice. Cover with the overhanging cling film. Put a small plate or saucer on top to fit inside the rim of the bowl, then stand a couple of heavy cans on top to press it down. Chill in the refrigerator for at least 10 minutes, or until you are ready to eat (it will keep for up to 24 hours).

PER SERVING 201 kcals, protein 5g, carbs 46g, fat 1g, sat fat trace, fibre 5g, sugar 11g, salt 0.6g

Tiramisu trifle

Everyone will fall in love with this recipe! It's hard to believe that something that tastes this good can take so little time and effort to make.

 10–15 minutes, plus chilling   8–10

- 300ml/½ pint strong good-quality black coffee
- 175ml/6fl oz Disaronno (amaretto) liqueur
- 500g tub mascarpone
- 500g/1lb 2oz good-quality fresh custard
- 250g/9oz Savoiardi biscuits (Italian sponge fingers) or sponge fingers
- 85g/3oz good-quality dark chocolate, roughly chopped

TO DECORATE
- 4 tbsp toasted slivered almonds
- chopped dark chocolate

1 Mix the coffee and liqueur in a wide dish. Beat the mascarpone and custard together in a bowl with a hand blender or whisk.

2 Take a third of the biscuits and dip each one into the coffee mix until soft but not soggy. Line the bottom of a glass trifle dish with the soaked biscuits and drizzle over a little more of the coffee mixture.

3 Sprinkle a third of the chocolate over the biscuits, then follow with a layer of the mascarpone mixture. Repeat twice more. Chill in the fridge for at least 2 hours (preferably overnight). Sprinkle with the almonds and chocolate before serving.

PER SERVING (8) 624 kcals, protein 8g, carbs 54g, fat 39g, sat fat 23g, fibre 1g, sugar 35g, salt 0.38g

Plum & marzipan tarte Tatin

Choose firm plums for this recipe – if they are overripe they will ooze too much juice and you will have a flood on your kitchen worktop.

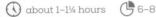 about 1–1¼ hours   6–8

- 25g/1oz butter
- 25g/1oz golden caster sugar
- 800g/1lb 12oz firm plums, not too ripe, halved and stoned
- 100g/4oz golden marzipan
- 40g/1½oz ground almonds
- 500g pack puff pastry, thawed if frozen
- pouring cream (single or double), to serve

1 Heat oven to 200C/180C fan/gas 6. Melt the butter in a 28cm tarte Tatin tin over a medium heat. Tip in the sugar and 1 tablespoon water and stir for a few minutes until lightly browned. Remove from the heat and put in the plums, cut-side up.

2 Chop the marzipan into as many chunks as there are plum halves, put a chunk into each plum and sprinkle over the ground almonds.

3 Roll out the pastry and trim to 4cm/1½in larger than the tin all round. Lift the pastry on to the tin and tuck it down between the plums and the inside of the tin. Bake for 30–35 minutes until the pastry is risen, crisp and golden. Cool for 10 minutes, then put a large flat plate with a rim over the tin. Holding it over the sink in case of drips, invert the tarte on to the plate. Serve with cream.

PER SERVING (6) 511 kcals, protein 8g, carbs 58g, fat 29g, sat fat 3g, fibre 3g, sugar 13g, salt 0.75g

Tropical-fruit salad

The lovely colours and fabulous flavours of this one-pot pudding will really surprise you.

 25–30 minutes   4

- 1 ripe papaya
- 1 small pineapple
- 12 cape gooseberries (physalis)
- 50g/2oz butter
- 4 tbsp light or dark muscovado sugar
- 4 tbsp coconut rum (or white or dark rum) or pineapple and coconut juice
- seeds 1 pomegranate
- vanilla or rum and raisin ice cream, to serve

1 Halve the papaya lengthways and scoop out the seeds, then peel the fruit and cut into slim wedges. Cut off the top, bottom and skin of the pineapple, and remove all the eyes from the flesh. Cut the pineapple lengthways into wedges and slice the core off the edge of each wedge. Cut each wedge crossways into chunks. Remove the papery husks from the cape gooseberries.

2 Melt the butter and sugar in a wide deep pan, add the prepared fruit and toss until coated and glistening. Sprinkle over the rum or fruit juice and the pomegranate seeds, and shake the pan to distribute evenly. Serve hot, with ice cream.

PER SERVING 308 kcals, protein 2g, carbs 45g, fat 11g, sat fat 7g, fibre 5g, sugar 15g, salt 0.22g

Cherry vanilla clafoutis

Serve the clafoutis barely warm to get the best from the subtle flavours.

 1–1¼ hours 6

- 650g/1lb 7oz fresh cherries (dark, juicy ones)
- butter, for greasing
- 4 tbsp golden caster sugar
- 4 tbsp kirsch
- 3 eggs
- 50g/2oz plain flour
- 200ml tub crème fraîche (full or half-fat)
- 1 tsp vanilla extract
- 150ml/¼ pint milk
- icing sugar, for dusting

1 Heat oven to 190C/170C fan/gas 5. Stone the cherries, but try to keep them whole.
2 Scatter the cherries over the base of a buttered shallow ovenproof dish, about 1 litre capacity. Sprinkle the cherries with 1 tablespoon each of the sugar and kirsch.
3 Whisk the eggs with an electric beater or hand whisk until they are soft and foamy – about 1–2 minutes. Whisk in the flour and remaining sugar, then add the remaining kirsch, the crème fraîche, vanilla extract and milk to make a batter.
4 Pour the batter over the cherries and bake fo 35–40 minutes until pale golden. Leave to cool to room temperature, then dust lightly with icing sugar and serve just warm.

PER SERVING 309 kcals, protein 7g, carbs 35g, fat 14g, sat fat 7g, fibre 1g, sugar 15g, salt 0.23g

Sticky cinnamon figs

Splash a few tablespoons of Armagnac or brandy over the figs before grilling to make a boozy pudding.

 10 minutes 4

- 8 ripe figs
- large knob butter
- 4 tbsp clear honey
- handful shelled pistachio nuts or whole almonds, chopped
- 1 tsp ground cinnamon or mixed spice
- mascarpone or Greek yogurt, to serve

1 Heat grill to medium–high. Cut a deep cross in the top of each fig, then ease the top apart like a flower. Sit the figs in a baking dish and drop a small piece of the butter into the centre of each fruit. Drizzle the honey over the figs, then sprinkle with the nuts and spice.

2 Grill for 5 minutes until the figs are softened and the honey and butter make a sticky sauce in the bottom of the dish. Serve warm, with dollops of mascarpone or yogurt.

PER SERVING 162 kcals, protein 3g, carbs 23g, fat 7g, sat fat 2g, fibre 2g, sugar 12g, salt 0.06g

Grilled summer berry pudding

· · · · · · · · · · · · · · · · · · · ·

This recipe has all the elements of a summer pudding but is much simpler, and served hot. The jammy smells as it cooks are wonderful.

 20–30 minutes   4

- 4 slices white sliced bread, crusts removed
- 85g/3oz golden caster sugar
- 2 tsp cornflour
- 200g tub low-fat fromage frais
- 300g/10oz mixed summer berries (such as raspberries, blueberries, redcurrants, sliced strawberries), defrosted if frozen

1 Heat grill to high. Lay the slices of bread slightly overlapping in a shallow flameproof dish. Sprinkle about 2 tablespoons of the sugar over the bread and grill for about 2 minutes until the bread is toasted and the sugar is starting to caramelise. Mix the cornflour into the fromage frais.

2 Heap the fruit on top of the bread and sprinkle with 1 more tablespoon of the sugar. Drop spoonfuls of the fromage-frais mixture on top, then sprinkle over the rest of the sugar.

3 Put the dish as close to the heat as you can and grill for 6–8 minutes until the fromage frais has browned and everything else is starting to bubble and turn juicy. Leave for a minute or two before serving.

· ·

PER SERVING 211 kcals, protein 7g, carbs 47g, fat 1g, sat fat none, fibre 2g, sugar 22g, salt 0.45g

Spicy steamed fruit pudding

This special treat of a dessert makes a good alternative to Christmas pudding. Serve it with crème fraîche or vanilla ice cream.

 3 hours   8–10

- 1 cup raisins
- 1 cup sultanas
- 1 cup self-raising flour
- 1 cup finely grated cold butter (about 100g/4oz), plus extra at room temperature for greasing
- 1 cup fresh brown breadcrumbs (about 4 thick slices bread)
- 1 cup light muscovado sugar
- 1 cup mixed nuts, chopped (optional)
- 1 tsp ground cinnamon
- 1 tsp ground mixed spice
- 1 cup milk
- 1 egg
- butterscotch or caramel sauce, to drizzle (optional)
- handful mixed nuts, to decorate (optional)

1 Using a 300ml/½ pint coffee mug as your cup measure, empty the first 6 cups and the nuts, if using, into a bowl with the spices, then stir in the milk and egg until well combined. Tip into a buttered 1.5 litre pudding bowl.
2 Cover with a double layer of buttered foil, making a pleat in the centre to allow the pudding to rise. Tie with string, then put in a steamer or large pan with enough gently simmering water to come halfway up the sides of the bowl. Cover and steam for 2½ hours, adding more water as necessary.
3 To serve, unwrap the pudding and invert on to a deep plate, then drizzle with sauce and decorate the top with nuts, if using.

PER SERVING (8) 423 kcals, protein 6g, carbs 75g, fat 13g, sat fat 7.9g, fibre 2g, sugar 29g, salt 0.7g

Index

almond, carrot & chickpea
  pilaf 158–9
apricot, chickpea, squash &
  guinea fowl tagine 182–3

bacon
  creamy, penne, & chicken
  36–7
  fish o'leekie 90–1
  & leek oven-baked risotto
  82–3
  lentil, sherry & guinea fowl
  46–7
  oven-baked risotto 86–7
balti, mixed veg 154–5
bean(s)
  & beef hotpot 180–1
  cannellini, soup 24–5
  & chicken stew 84–5
  chipotle, chilli, & baked eggs
  152–3
  green, chicken & ginger 48–9
  lemon & fish 104–5
  & pasta stew with meatballs
  60–1
  pinto, & squid stew 106–7
  & spicy sausage 74–5
  squash & lentils 140–1
  Sunday brunch 52–3
  white, soup, with chilli oil 30–1
beef
  & bean hotpot 180–1
  Chinese-style braised 168–9
  corned, Sunday brunch 52–3

Mexican chilli 184–5
  paprikash 186–7
berries
  Beaujolais 192–3
  grilled summer pud 208–9
  simple summer pud 196–7
biryani, chicken 54–5
broccoli lemon chicken 50–1
bulghar pilaf & fish 98–9
butternut squash
  apricot, chickpea & guinea
  fowl tagine 182–3
  lentil & beans 140–1

carrot
  chickpea & almond pilaf
  158–9
  orange & veal 174–5
casserole, vegetarian 136–7
  & dumplings 144–5
celeriac & salmon bake 108–9
cheesy
  chop & chips 78–9
  veg hotpot 162–3
cherry vanilla clafoutis 204–5
chicken
  & bean stew 84–5
  biryani 54–5
  broccoli lemon 50–1
  & coconut Thai soup 18–19
  & creamy bacon penne
  36–7
  curry 40–1
  curry in a hurry 58–9

fragrant curry 188–9
  ginger & green bean hotpot
  48–9
  & goat's cheese 178–9
  Moroccan lemon 64–5
  pizza melts 80–1
  roast ratatouille 32–3
  spring, paella 70–1
  & spring veg 166–7
  & spring veg stew 76–7
  Thai green curry 172–3
  & thyme bake 44–5
chickpea
  almond & carrot pilaf 158–9
  & chorizo soup 12–13
  Moroccan soup 28–9
  squash, apricot & guinea fowl
  tagine 182–3
chilli
  chipotle bean, & eggs 152–3
  lime & scallop 124–5
  Marrakech 164–5
  Mexican beef 184–5
chips
  cheesy 78–9
  & egg, oven 156–7
chorizo
  & chickpea soup 12–13
  fish, lemon & beans 104–5
  potato & haddock 102–3
  & prawn spicy rice 130–1
cider, parsnip & pork 176–7
cinnamon sticky fig 206–7
clafoutis, cherry vanilla 204–5

oconut & chicken Thai soup
18–19
od, sizzling summer 120–1
ookie-dough crumble 194–5
ourgette & prawn curry 100–1
rumble, cookie-dough 194–5
urry
chicken 188–9
courgette & prawn 100–1
curried rice & spinach 142–3
home-style chicken 40–1
in a hurry 58–9
Kerala prawn 114–15
mixed veg balti 154–5
Thai green chicken 172–3

umplings 144–5

gg
baked, & chipotle bean chilli
152–3
& chips, oven 156–7
poached, & ratatouille 148–9

g
raita 140–1
sticky cinnamon 206–7
h
Italian-style roast 112–13
with lemon & beans 104–5
o'leekie 90–1
& spiced bulghar pilaf 98–9
uit
tropical, salad 202–3
spicy steamed pud 210–11
h, see also haddock; salmon;
sea bass; cod

inger, green bean & chicken

hotpot 48–9
goat's cheese & chicken
178–9
guinea fowl
pot-roast, with lentils, sherry &
bacon 46–7
tagine, with chickpeas,
squash & apricots 182–3

haddock
chorizo, & new potato 102–3
creamy, & tatties 122
smoked, chowder 14–15
smoked, stovies 126–7
in tomato basil sauce 88–9

jambalaya, sausage & prawn
128–9

lamb
chilli Marrakech 164–5
fruit tagine 38–9
hob-to-table moussaka 170–1
& Mediterranean veg 56–7
& red pepper stew 190–1
Turkish pilaf 68–9
leek
& bacon oven-baked risotto
82–3
fish o'leekie 90–1
& salmon 132–3
& sausage hash 42–3
lemon
& beans with fish 104–5
broccoli chicken 50–1
Moroccan chicken 64–5
lentil(s)
bean & squash spice-pot
140–1

sherry, bacon & guinea fowl
46–7

marzipan plum tarte tatin 200–1
meatballs, with bean & pasta
stew 60–1
moussaka, hob-to-table 170–1
mozzarella potato tortilla 138–9
mussel(s)
creamy spiced 116–17
& sea bass Italian pot 94–5

noodle(s), chilli prawn 96–7

omelette, Greek salad 146–7
orange
carrot & veal 174–5
olives, bay & pork 34–5

paella, spring chicken 70–1
paprikash, beef 186–7
parsnip, cider & pork 176–7
pasta
20-min seafood 134–5
& bean stew, with meatballs
60–1
creamy bacon, & chicken
36–7
pepper, red, & lamb stew 190–1
pilaf, carrot, chickpea &
almond 158–9
pilaf
prawn 92–3
spring veg 150–1
Turkish lamb 68–9
pizza chicken melts 80–1
plum marzipan tarte tatin 200–1
pork
cheesy chop, & chips 78–9

Chinese broth 26–7
orange, olives & bay 34–5
slow-braised shoulder, with
    cider & parsnips 176–7
spiced, & stir-fried greens 72–3
summer, & potatoes 62–3
potato
chips 78–9, 156–7
& creamy haddock 122
& mozzarella tortilla 138–9
new, chorizo, & haddock
    102–3
smoked-haddock stovies
    126–7
& summer pork 62–3
prawn
chilli noodles 96–7
& chorizo spicy rice 130–1
& courgette curry 100–1
Kerala curry 114–15
pilaf 92–3
& sausage jambalaya 128–9
& sea bass Italian pot 94–5
Thai fried rice 110–11

raita, fig 140–1
ratatouille
& poached egg 148–9
roast chicken 32–3
rice
chicken biryani 54–5
curried, & spinach 142–3
fish o'leekie 90–1
sausage & prawn jambalaya
    128–9
spicy prawn & chorizo 130–1
spring chicken paella 70–1
Thai prawn fried 110–11
see also pilaf; risotto

risotto
oven-baked 86–7
oven-baked leek & bacon
    82–3
seafood 118–19

salad
Greek, omelette 146–7
tropical fruit 202–3
salmon
& leeks 132–3
smoked, & celeriac bake
    108–9
sausage
& beans, spicy 74–5
frying-pan hotpot 66–7
& leek hash 42–3
meatballs 60–1
& prawn jambalaya 128–9
scallop, chilli & lime 124–5
sea bass & seafood Italian stew
    94–5
seafood
20-min pasta 134–5
risotto 118–19
& sea bass 94–5
see also prawn
soup
autumn vegetable 16–17
cannellini bean 24–5
Chinese pork 26–7
chorizo & chickpea 12–13
chunky winter broth 10–11
Moroccan chickpea 28–9
Provençal tomato 20–1
smoked haddock chowder
    14–15
Thai chicken coconut 18–19
three green veg 22–3

white bean, chilli oil 30–1
spinach & curried rice 142–3
squid
& pinto bean stew 106–7
& sea bass stew 94–5
stew
bean & pasta 60–1
chicken & bean 84–5
chicken & spring veg 76–7
lamb & red pepper 190–1
squid & pinto bean 106–7
stir-fried greens 72–3
strawberry, Beaujolais 192–3
summer pudding
grilled berry 208–9
simple 196–7

tagine
fruity lamb 38–9
guinea fowl 182–3
tarte tatin, plum marzipan
    200–1
tiramisu trifle 198–9
toasts, garlic 106–7
tofu & summer veg bowl 160–1
tomato
basil sauce 88–9
Provençal soup 20–1
tortilla, potato mozzarella 138–
trifle, tiramisu 198–9

vanilla cherry clafoutis 204–5
veal, carrot, & orange 174–5

Also available from BBC Books and Good Food

Baking
Bakes & Cakes
Chocolate Treats
Cupcakes & Small Bakes
Easy Baking Recipes
Fruity Puds
Teatime Treats
Tempting Desserts
Traybakes
Easy
30-minute suppers
Budget Dishes
Cheap Eats
Easy Student Dinners
Easy Weeknight Suppers
More One-pot Dishes
More Slow Cooker
  Favourites
Pressure Cooker Favourites
Simple Suppers

Speedy Suppers
Slow Cooker Favourites
Everyday
Best-ever Chicken Recipes
Best-ever Curries
Fish & Seafood Dishes
Gluten-free Recipes
Healthy Family Food
Hot & Spicy Dishes
Italian Feasts
Low-carb Cooking
Meals for Two
Mediterranean Dishes
Pasta & Noodle Dishes
Picnics & Packed Lunches
Recipes for Kids
Storecupboard Suppers
Healthy
Healthy Chicken Recipes
Healthy Eats

Low-calorie Recipes
Low-fat Feasts
More Low-fat Feasts
Seasonal Salads
Superhealthy Suppers
Veggie Dishes
Weekend
Barbecues and Grills
Christmas Dishes
Delicious Gifts
Dinner-party Dishes
Make Ahead Meals
Slow-cooking Recipes
Soups & Sides
Sunday Lunches